Ruskin Bond was born in Kasauli in 1934, and grew up in Jamnagar, Dehra Dun and Simla. In the course of a writing career spanning four decades, he has written over a hundred short stories, essays and novels and more than thirty books for children. He has also edited three anthologies for Penguin Books.

His first novel, *The Room on the Roof*, written when he was seventeen, received the John Llewellyn Rhys Memorial Prize in 1957. In 1992, for *Our Trees Still Grow in Dehra*, he received the Sahitya Akademi Award for English writing in India. In 1995, Penguin Books published *The Complete Stories and Novels*, making him one of ten authors to be so honoured. A 26-episode serial based on his short stories was recently telecast by Doordarshan. *Scenes from a Writer's Life* is his first full-fledged memoir, recounting his formative years.

Ruskin Bond lives in Mussoorie.

Ruskin Bond

Scenes from a Writer's Life

PENGUIN BOOKS

Penguin Books India (P) Ltd, 11 Community Centre, Panchsheel Park, New Delhi-110017, India
Penguin Books Ltd., 27 Wrights Lane, London W8 5TZ, UK
Penguin Books USA Inc., 375 Hudson Street, New York, NY 10014, USA
Penguin Books Australia Ltd., Ringwood, Victoria, Australia
Penguin Books Canada Ltd., 10 Alcorn Avenue, Suite 300, Toronto, Ontario M4V 3B2, Canada
Penguin Books (NZ) Ltd., 182-190 Wairau Road, Auckland 10, New Zealand

First published by Penguin Books India (P) Ltd. 1997

10 9 8 7 6 5 4 3 2

Typeset in New Centurybook by Digital Technologies and Printing Solutions, New Delhi

For you, my gentle reader

For you, my gentle reader.

Contents

Acknowledgements

Dr Howard Gotlieb, Director of Boston University's Special Collections Library, for enabling me to use the correspondence in 'Notes and Letters'.

Anuradha Dutt, of Penguin Books India, for her editorial help.

The BBC, for its abridged version of the chapter, 'The Playing Fields of Simla,' broadcast during its India 1997 Season.

'I think it may have been bad luck that your first book came to you so early, making a long wait afterwards inevitable—but that doesn't invalidate the first book. *The Room on the Roof* remains just what it always was: a remarkably *true* piece of writing (than which what more could anyone ask for?). Your snag is, surely, that you are a writer who works best from very close to your own experience—which means that one is terribly dependent on the nature of one's experience. Only so much that is of general validity happens to one—and only so much of what happens to one strikes down to the level from which one writes. I sometimes feel very envious of people with the other kind of mind, full of invention. But I still like best the kind of writing which goes inwards rather than outwards.'

Diana Athill in a letter to
the author, 23 March 1964

Preamble, Prelude, Prologue

Few people bother to read Forewords, Introductions, or Prefaces, and I can't say I blame them. The very names are off-putting. Like speeches they are best left to die away on the wind, for in cold print all that fine rhetoric looks uninviting and indigestible. I don't know of anyone who reads volumes of speeches, and I have yet to meet someone who has read the Introductions to the world's classics. So why read mine?

I shall be crafty and call it something else.

The reader may be surprised to know that this is the first time I am attempting straight autobiography. True, the autobiographical element is present in much of my work, but there is really more fiction in my fiction than the reader may realize. That dramatic escape from Java, those supernatural experiences, and the close encounters with bears, leopards and amorous pythons have a certain verisimilitude because I have used the first person and taken the trouble to make the backgrounds and episodes convincing. I'm no Baron Munchausen, but sometimes I have given rein to my imagination, although in a perfectly credible way.

According to to my mother, my grandfather did keep a number of interesting pets, and I have described them and their activities in some of my tales. But I have not tried to emulate him in this respect. Visitors to my small flat in Mussoorie are sometimes disappointed to find that there are no flying foxes hanging from the ceiling or white mice peeping out from under the cushions. Mukesh (a member of my family) did on one occasion bring home a guinea pig, and we kept it for a few days. But guinea pigs, like their relatives, the rabbits, evacuate their food as rapidly as they consume it (which is all day) and cleaning up the mess is a full-time job. We gave the guinea pig to one of the many NGOs that has sprung up on the hillside. They were looking for a fund-raising mascot.

I love animals but their bowel movements are somewhat different from ours, and they were never meant to live in an author's bedroom, library or clothes cupboard. Their true home is in the wild, where they can enrich the soil rather than the carpet.

So the reader who comes to this book looking for my fictional persona will be disappointed. I am not an eccentric recluse who converses with rhesus monkeys. I do not care for rhesus monkeys. They invade my rooms, wreck the telephone, raid the kitchen and fling my geraniums out of the window. No, I am like any other normal human being who pays his taxes and curses when the lights go out.

*

The first twenty-one years of my life form the period covered by this memoir. Although, for most of us, these are not years of great achievement, they are the formative years, and the most emotional, impressionable, vulnerable years. There are struggles, setbacks, failures, but hope and optimism have not been blighted, and the cynicism of middle age is yet far distant.

I was still a pimply adolescent when I decided I wanted to be a writer. I had read Dickens' *David Copperfield* and Hugh Walpole's *Fortitude* and decided that I wanted to be like the writer-heroes of both books. Before that, my father had brought me up on a diet of the children's classics as well as other forms of entertainment, and although I was only ten when he died, the seed had been sown and I had begun to dream. The ensuing lonely period with my mother and stepfather only cemented my attachment to the world of books. They were the great escape. And as I grew out of my teens I began to love the country that I had, till then, taken for granted—to love it through the friends I made and through the mountains, valleys, fields and forests which had made an indelible impression on my mind (for India is an atmosphere as much as it is a land)—with the result that, no sooner had I set foot in the West, than I wanted to return to India and to all that I had known and loved.

It was only by going away that I came to the realization that I would never go away again, no matter what happened. This was where I belonged and this was where I would stay, come flood or fury.

So this is the story of two journeys—one, to the point where I had found a publisher for my first book and could confidently say, 'I am an author'; and the other, to the point where I had resolved most of my inner conflicts and could confidently say, 'I am an Indian'—in the broadest, all-embracing, all-Indian sense of the word.

Being a child of changing times, I had grown up with divided loyalties; but at the end of the journey I had come to realize that I was blessed with a double inheritance. And I was determined to make the most of it.

If it were not for the family that has grown up around me, making me a prisoner of love, I doubt if I would have remained rooted to one place for so long—Mussoorie and its surroundings.

In 1970 there came Prem and his young wife. Then their children, Rakesh, Mukesh and Savitri. Rakesh grew up and married, and he and Beena presented us with two delightful youngsters—Siddharth and Shrishti. So there is no escape. I have become a family man by virtue of remaining a bachelor. In many ways, this is the ideal situation for a writer. All the noise, merriment and bedlam of a large family living together has become an integral part of my own life, and for the most part it's joy to my heart and music to my ears.

And for me, it makes up for the lonely childhood years when I felt distanced from family and could find happiness only in the homes of friends or between the covers of books.

The painful but sometimes pleasurable process of growing up and becoming a writer is described in these pages.

Ruskin Bond

Chapter One

Life with Father

During my childhood and early boyhood with my father, we were never in one house or dwelling for very long. I think the 'Tennis Bungalow' in Jamnagar (in the grounds of the Ram Vilas Palace) housed us for a couple of years, and that was probably the longest period.

In Jamnagar itself we had at least three abodes—a rambling, leaking old colonial mansion called 'Cambridge House'; a wing of an old palace, the Lal Bagh I think it was called, which was also inhabited by bats and cobras; and the aforementioned 'Tennis Bungalow,' a converted sports pavilion which was really quite bright and airy.

I think my father rather enjoyed changing houses, setting up home in completely different surroundings. He loved rearranging rooms too, so that this month's sitting room became next month's bedroom, and so on; furniture would also be moved around quite frequently, somewhat to my mother's irritation, for she liked having things in their familiar places. She had grown up in one abode (her father's Dehra house) whereas my father hadn't remained anywhere for very long. Sometimes he spoke of making a home in Scotland, beside Loch Lomond, but it was only a

1

distant dream.

The only real stability was represented by his stamp collection, and this he carried around in a large tin trunk, for it was an extensive and valuable collection—there was an album for each country he specialized in: Greece, Newfoundland, British possessions in the Pacific, Borneo, Zanzibar, Sierra Leone; these were some of the lands whose stamps he favoured most . . .

I did share some of his enthusiasm for stamps, and they gave me a strong foundation in geography and political history, for he went to the trouble of telling me something about the places and people depicted on them—that Pitcairn Island was inhabited largely by mutineers from *H.M.S.Bounty*; that the Solomon Islands were famous for their butterflies; that Britannia still ruled the waves (but only just); that Iraq had a handsome young boy king; that in Zanzibar the Sultan wore a fez; that zebras were exclusive to Kenya, Uganda and Tanganyika; that in America presidents were always changing; and that the handsome young hero on Greek stamps was a Greek god with a sore heel. All this and more, I remember from my stamp-sorting sessions with my father. However, it did not form a bond between him and my mother. She was bored with the whole thing.

*

My earliest memories don't come in any particular order, but most of them pertain to Jamnagar, where we lived until I was five or six years old.

There was the beach at Balachadi, and I remember picking up seashells and wanting to collect them much as my father collected stamps. When the tide was out I went paddling with some of the children from the palace.

My father set up a schoolroom for the palace children. It was on the ground floor of a rambling old palace, which had a tower and a room on the top. Sometimes I attended my father's classes more as an observer than a scholar. One day I set off on my own to explore the deserted palace, and ascended some wandering steps to the top, where I found myself in a little room full of tiny stained-glass windows. I took turns at each window pane, looking out at a green or red or yellow world. It was a magical room.

Many years later—almost forty years later, in fact—I wrote a story with this room as its setting. It was called *The Room of Many Colours** and it had in it a mad princess, a gardener and a snake.

*

Not all memories are dream-like and idyllic. I witnessed my parents' quarrels from an early age, and later when they resulted in my mother taking off for unknown destinations (unknown to me). I would feel helpless and insecure. My father's hand was always there, and I held it firmly until it was wrenched away by the angel of death.

That early feeling of insecurity was never to leave me, and in adult life, when I witnessed quarrels between people who were close to me, I was always deeply disturbed—more for the children, whose lives were bound to be affected by such emotional discord. But can it be helped? People who marry young, even those who are in

---

* In *Time Stops at Shamli and Other Stories*.

love, do not really know each other. The body chemistry may be right but the harmony of two minds is what makes relationships endure.

Words of wisdom from a disappointed bachelor!

I don't suppose I would have written so much about childhood or even about other children if my own childhood had been all happiness and light. I find that those who have had contented, normal childhoods, seldom remember much about them; nor do they have much insight into the world of children. Some of us are born sensitive. And, if, on top of that, we are pulled about in different directions (both emotionally and physically), we might just end up becoming writers.

No, we don't become writers in schools of creative writing. We become writers before we learn to write. The rest is simply learning how to put it all together.

*

I learnt to read from my father but not in his classroom.

The children were older than me. Four of them were princesses, very attractive, but always clad in buttoned-up jackets and trousers. This was a bit confusing for me, because I had at first taken them for boys. One of them used to pinch my cheeks and hug me. While I thought she was a boy, I rather resented the familiarity. When I discovered she was a girl (I had to be told), I wanted more of it.

I was shy of these boyish princesses, and was to remain shy of girls until I was in my teens.

*

4

Between Tennis Bungalow and the palace were lawns and flower beds. One of my earliest memories is of picking my way through a forest of flowering cosmos; to a five-year-old they were almost trees, the flowers nodding down at me in friendly invitation.

Since then, the cosmos has been my favourite flower—fresh, open, uncomplicated—living up to its name, *cosmos,* the universe as an ordered whole. White, purple and rose, they are at their best in each other's company, growing almost anywhere, in the hills or on the plains, in Europe or tropical America. Waving gently in the softest of breezes, they are both sensuous and beyond sensuality. An early influence!

There were of course rose bushes in the palace grounds, kept tidy and trim and looking very like those in the illustrations in my first copy of *Alice in Wonderland*, a well-thumbed edition from which my father often read to me. (Not the Tennial illustrations, something a little softer.) I think I have read *Alice* more often than any other book, with the possible exception of *The Diary of a Nobody*, which I turn to whenever I am feeling a little low. Both books help me to a better appreciation of the absurdities of life.

There were extensive lawns in front of the bungalow, where I could romp around or push my small sister around on a tricycle. She was a backward child, who had been affected by polio and some damage to the brain (having been born prematurely and delivered with the help of forceps), and she was the cross that had to be borne by my parents, together and separately. In spite of her infirmities, Ellen was going to outlive most of us.

*

Although we lived briefly in other houses, and even for a time in the neighbouring state of Pithadia, Tennis Bungalow was our home for most of the time we were in Jamnagar.

There were several Englishmen working for the Jam Saheb. The port authority was under Commander Bourne, a retired British naval officer. And a large farm (including a turkey farm) was run for the state by a Welsh couple, the Jenkins. I remember the verandah of the Jenkins home, because the side table was always stacked with copies of the humorous weekly, *Punch*, mailed regularly to them from England. I was too small to read *Punch*, but I liked looking at the drawings.

The Bournes had a son who was at school in England, but he had left his collection of comics behind, and these were passed on to me. Thus I made the acquaintance of Korky the Kat, Tiger Tim, Desperate Dan, Our Wullie and other comic-paper heroes of the late thirties.

There was one cinema somewhere in the city, and English-language films were occasionally shown. My first film was very disturbing for me, because the hero was run through with a sword. This was Noel Coward's operetta, *Bitter Sweet*, in which Nelson Eddy and Jennette MacDonald made love in duets. My next film was *Tarzan of the Apes*, in which Johny Weissmuller, the Olympic swimmer, gave Maureen O'Sullivan, pretty and petite, a considerable mauling in their treetop home. But it was to be a few years before I became a movie buff.

Looking up one of my tomes of Hollywood history, I note that *Bitter Sweet* was released in 1940, so that was probably our last year in Jamnagar. My father must have been over forty when he joined the Royal Air Force (RAF), to do his bit for King and country. He may have bluffed his age (he was born in 1896), but perhaps you could enlist in your mid-forties during the War. He was given the rank of pilot officer and assigned to the cipher section of Air Headquarters in New Delhi. So there was a Bond working in Intelligence long before the fictional James arrived on the scene.

The War wasn't going too well for England in 1941, and it wasn't going too well for me either, for I found myself interned in a convent school in the hill station of Mussoorie. I hated it from the beginning. The nuns were strict and unsympathetic; the food was awful (stringy meat boiled with pumpkins); the boys were for the most part dull and unfriendly, the girls too subdued; and the latrines were practically inaccessible. We had to bathe in our underwear, presumably so that the nuns would not be distracted by the sight of our undeveloped sex! I had to endure this place for over a year because my father was being moved around from Calcutta to Delhi to Karachi, and my mother was already engaged in her affair with my future stepfather. At times I thought of running away, but where was I to run?

Picture postcards from my father brought me some cheer. These postcards formed part of Lawson Wood's 'Granpop' series—'Granpop' being an ape of sorts, who indulged in various human activities, such as attending cocktail parties and dancing to Scottish bagpipes. 'Is this how you feel now that the rains are here?' my father had written under one illustration of 'Granpop' doing the rumba in a tropical downpour.

I enjoyed getting these postcards, with the messages from my father saying that books and toys and stamps were waiting for me when I came home. I preserved them for fifty years, and now they are being looked after by Dr Howard Gotlieb in my archives at Boston University's Mugar Memorial Library. My own letters can perish, but not those postcards!

I have no cherished memories of life at the convent school. It wasn't a cruel place but it lacked character of any kind; it was really a conduit for boys and girls going on to bigger schools in the hill station. I am told that today it has a beautiful well-stocked library, but that the children are not allowed to use the books lest they soil them; everything remains as tidy and spotless as the nuns' habits.

One day in mid-term my mother turned up unexpectedly and withdrew me from the school. I was overjoyed but also a little puzzled by this sudden departure. After all, no one had really taken me seriously when I'd said I hated the place.

Oddly enough, we did not stop in Dehra Dun at my grandmother's place. Instead my mother took me straight to the railway station and put me on the night train to Delhi. I don't remember if anyone accompanied me—I must have been too young to travel alone—but I remember being met at the Delhi station by my father in full uniform. It was early summer, and he was in khakis, but the blue RAF cap took my fancy. Come winter, he'd be wearing a dark blue uniform with a different kind of cap, and by then he'd be a flying officer and getting saluted by juniors. Being wartime, everyone was saluting madly, and I soon developed the habit, saluting everyone in sight.

8

An uncle on my mother's side, Fred Clark, was then the station superintendent at Delhi railway station, and he took us home for breakfast to his bungalow, not far from the station. From the conversation that took place during the meal I gathered that my parents had separated, that my mother was remaining in Dehra Dun, and that henceforth I would be in my father's custody. My sister Ellen was to stay with 'Calcutta Granny'—my father's seventy-year-old mother. The arrangement pleased me, I must admit.

*

The two years I spent with my father were probably the happiest of my childhood—although, for him, they must have been a period of trial and tribulation. Frequent bouts of malaria had undermined his constitution; the separation from my mother weighed heavily on him, and it could not be reversed; and at the age of eight I was self-willed and demanding.

He did his best for me, dear man. He gave me his time, his companionship, his complete attention.

A year was to pass before I was re-admitted to a boarding school, and I would have been quite happy never to have gone to school again. My year in the convent had been sufficient punishment for uncommitted sins. I felt that I had earned a year's holiday.

It was a glorious year, during which we changed our residence at least four times—from a tent on a flat treeless plain outside Delhi, to a hutment near Humayun's tomb; to a couple of rooms on Atul Grove Road; to a small flat on Hailey Road; and finally to an apartment in Scindia

House, facing the Connaught Circus.

We were not very long in the tent and hutment—but long enough for me to remember the scorching winds of June, and the *bhisti's* hourly visit to douse the *khas-khas* matting with water. This turned a hot breeze into a refreshing, fragrant zephyr—for about half an hour. And then the dust and the prickly heat took over again. A small table fan was the only luxury.

Except for Sundays, I was alone during most of the day; my father's office in Air Headquarters was somewhere near India Gate. He'd return at about six, tired but happy to find me in good spirits. For although I had no friends during that period, I found plenty to keep me occupied—books, stamps, the old gramophone, hundreds of postcards which he'd collected during his years in England, a scrapbook, albums of photographs . . . And sometimes I'd explore the jungle behind the tents; but I did not go very far, because of the snakes that proliferated there.

I would have my lunch with a family living in a neighbouring tent, but at night my father and I would eat together. I forget who did the cooking. But he made the breakfast, getting up early to whip up some fresh butter (he loved doing this) and then laying the table with corn-flakes or grapenuts, and eggs poached or fried.

The gramophone was a great companion when my father was away. He had kept all the records he had collected in Jamnagar, and these were added to from time to time. There were operatic arias and duets from *La Bohème* and *Madame Butterfly*; ballads and traditional airs rendered by Paul Robeson, Peter Dawson, Richard Crooks, Webster Booth, Nelson Eddy and other tenors and baritones, and of course the great Russian bass, Chaliapin. And there were lighter, music-hall songs and comic relief provided by Gracie Fields (the 'Lancashire Lass'), George Formby with his ukelele, Arthur Askey ('big-hearted' Arthur—he was a tiny chap,) Flanagan and Allan, and a host of other recording artistes. You couldn't just put on some music and lie back and enjoy it. That was the day of the wind-up gramophone, and it had to be wound up fairly vigorously before a 75 rmp record could be played. I enjoyed this chore. The needle, too, had to be changed after almost every record, if you wanted to keep them in decent condition. And the records had to be packed flat, otherwise, in the heat and humidity they were inclined to assume weird shapes and become unplayable.

It was always a delight to accompany my father to one of the record shops in Connaught Place, and come home with a new record by one of our favourite singers.

After a few torrid months in the tent-house and then in a brick hutment, which was even hotter, my father was permitted to rent rooms of his own on Atul Grove Road, a tree-lined lane not far from Connaught Place, which was then the hub and business centre of New Delhi. Keeping me with him had been quite unofficial; his superiors were always wanting to know why my mother wasn't around to look after me. He was really hoping that the war would end soon, so that he could take me to England and put me in a good school there. He had been selling some of his more valuable stamps and had put quite a bit in the bank.

One evening he came home with a bottle of Scotch whisky. This was most unusual, because I had never seen him drinking—not even beer. Had he suddenly decided to hit the bottle?

The mystery was solved when an American officer dropped in to have dinner with us (having a guest for dinner was a very rare event), and our cook excelled himself by producing succulent pork chops, other viands and vegetables, and my favourite chocolate pudding. Before we sat down to dinner, our guest polished off several pegs of whisky (my father had a drink too), and after dinner they sat down to go through some of my father's stamp albums. The American collector bought several stamps, and we went to bed richer by a couple of thousand rupees.

That it was possible to make money out of one's hobby was something I was to remember when writing became my passion.

When my father had a bad bout of malaria and was admitted to the Military Hospital, I was on my own for about ten days. Our immediate neighbours, an elderly Anglo-Indian couple, kept an eye on me, only complaining that I went through a tin of guava jam in one sitting. This tendency to over-indulge has been with me all my life. Those stringy convent meals must have had something to do with it.

I made one friend during the Atul Grove days. He was a boy called Joseph—from South India, I think—who lived next door. In the evenings we would meet on a strip of grassland across the road and engage in wrestling bouts which were watched by an admiring group of servants' children from a nearby hostelry. We also had a great deal of fun in the trenches that had been dug along the road in case of possible Japanese air raids (there had been one on Calcutta). During the monsoon they filled with rain-water, much to the delight of the local children, who used them as miniature swimming pools. They were then quite impracticable as air raid shelters.

Of course, the real war was being fought in Burma and the Far East, but Delhi was full of men in uniform. When winter came, my father's khakis were changed for dark blue RAF caps and uniforms, which suited him nicely. He was a good-looking man, always neatly dressed; on the short side but quite sturdy. He was over forty when he had joined up—hence the office job, deciphering (or helping to create) codes and ciphers. He was quite secretive about it all (as indeed he was supposed to be), and as he confided in me on almost every subject but his work, he was obviously a reliable Intelligence officer.

He did not have many friends in Delhi. There was the occasional visit to Uncle Fred near the railway station, and sometimes he'd spend a half-hour with Mr Rankin, who owned a large drapery shop at Connaught Circus, where officers' uniforms were tailored. Mr Rankin was another enthusiastic stamp collector, and the two of them would get together in Mr Rankin's back office and exchange stamps or discuss new issues. I think the drapery establishment closed down after the War. Mr Rankin was always extremely well dressed, as though he had stepped straight out of Saville Row and on to the steamy streets of Delhi.

My father and I explored old tombs and monuments, but going to the pictures was what we did most, if he was back from work fairly early.

Connaught Place was well served with cinemas—the Regal, Rivoli, Odeon and Plaza, all very new and shiny—and they exhibited the latest Hollywood and British productions. It was in these cinemas that I discovered the beautiful Sonja Henie, making love on skates and even getting married on ice; Nelson and Jeanette making love in duets; Errol Flynn making love on the high seas; and Gary Cooper and Claudette Colbert making love in the bedroom (*Bluebeard's Eighth Wife*). I made careful listings of all the films I saw, including their casts, and to this day I can give you the main performers in almost any film made in the 1940s. And I still think it was cinema's greatest decade, with the stress on good story, clever and economical direction (films seldom exceeded 120-minutes running time), superb black and white photography, and actors and actresses who were also personalities in their own right. The era of sadistic thrills, gore, and psychopathic killers was still far away. The accent was on entertainment—naturally enough, when the worst war in history had spread across Europe, Asia and the Pacific.

*

When my father broached the subject of sending me to a boarding school, I used every argument I could think of to dissuade him. The convent school was still fresh in my memory and I had no wish to return to any institution remotely resembling it—certainly not after almost a year of untrammelled freedom and my father's companionship.

'Why do you want to send me to school again?' I asked. 'I can learn more at home. I can read books, I can write letters, I can even do sums!'

'Not bad for a boy of nine,' said my father. 'But I can't teach you algebra, physics and chemistry.'

'I don't want to be a chemist.'

'Well, what would you like to be when you grow up?'

'A tap-dancer.'

'We've been seeing too many pictures. Everyone says I spoil you.'

I tried another argument. 'You'll have to live on your own again. You'll feel lonely.'

'That can't be helped, son. But I'll come to see you as often as I can. You see, they're posting me to Karachi for some time, and then I'll be moved again—they won't allow me to keep you with me at some of these places. Would you like to stay with your mother?'

I shook my head.

'With Calcutta Granny?'

'I don't know her.'

'When the War's over I'll take you with me to England. But for the next year or two we must stay here. I've found a nice school for you.'

'Another convent?'

'No, it's a prep school for boys in Simla. And I may be able to get posted there during the summer.'

'I want to see it first,' I said.

'We'll go up to Simla together. Not now—in April or May, before it gets too hot. It doesn't matter if you join school a bit later—I know you'll soon catch up with the others.'

There was a brief trip to Dehra Dun. I think my father felt that there was still a chance of a reconciliation with my mother. But her affair with the businessman was too far gone. His own wife had been practically abandoned and left to look after the photography shop she'd brought along with her dowry. She was a stout lady with high blood pressure, who once went in search of my mother and stepfather with an axe. Fortunately, they were not at home that day and she had to vent her fury on the furniture.

In later years, when I got to know her quite well, she told me that my father was a very decent man, who treated her with great courtesy and kindness on the one occasion they met.

I remember we stayed in a little hotel or boarding house just off the Eastern Canal Road.

Dehra was a green and leafy place. The houses were separated by hedges, not walls, and the residential areas were criss-crossed by little lanes bordered by hibiscus or oleander shrubs.

We were soon back in Delhi.

My parents' separation was final and it was to be almost two years before I saw my mother again.

Chapter Two
Simla and Delhi, 1943

We took the railcar to Simla. It was the nicest way of
travelling through the mountains. The narrow-gauge
train took twice as long and left you covered in soot. Going
up in a motor car made you nauseous. The railcar glided
smoothly round and up gradients, slipping through the
103 tunnels without subjecting the passengers to blasts
of hot black smoke.

We stopped at Barog, a pretty little wayside station,
famous for its breakfasts and in winter, for its mistletoe.
We got into Simla at lunch-time and dined at Davico's.
Simla was well-served by restaurants. Davico's was
famous for its meringues, and I experienced one for the
first time. Then we trudged off to a lodging house called
Craig Dhu, which was to be another of our temporary
homes.

The Bishop Cotton Prep School was situated in Chotta
Simla, at some distance from the Senior School. The boys
were at play when I first saw them from the road above
the playing field.

'You can see they're a happy lot,' said my father.

They certainly seemed a good deal noisier (and less

17

inhibited) than their counterparts at the Mussoorie convent. Some spun tops; others wrestled with each other; several boys were dashing about with butterfly nets, chasing a large blue butterfly. Three or four sat quietly on the steps, perusing comics. In those days you had story comics or papers, such as *Hotspur, Wizard* or *Champion*, and you had actually to read them.

It was to be a month before I joined the school (admission took time), and in the interim I enjoyed an idyllic holiday with my father. If Davico's had its meringues, Wenger's had its pastries and chocolate cakes, while at Kwality the curry puffs and ice creams were superb. The reader will consider me to have been a spoilt brat, and so I was for a time; but there was always the nagging fear that my father would be posted to some inaccessible corner of the country, and I would be left to rot in boarding school for the rest of my days.

During a rickshaw ride around Elysium Hill, my father told me Kipling's story of the phantom rickshaw—my first encounter with hill-station lore. He also showed me the shop where Kim got his training as a spy from the mysterious Lurgan Sahib. I had not read Kipling at the time, but through my father's retellings I was already familiar with many of his characters and settings. The same Lurgan Sahib (I learnt later) had inspired another novel, F. Marion Crawford's *Mr Isaacs*. A Bishop Cotton's boy, Richard Blaker, had written a novel called *Scabby Dixon*, which had depicted life in the school at the turn of the century. And Bishop Cotton, our founder, had himself been a young master at Rugby under the famous Dr Arnold who was to write *Tom Brown's Schooldays*. Cotton became the first headmaster at Marlborough before coming out to India.

All these literary traditions were beginning to crowd upon me. And of course there was the strange fact that my father had named me Ruskin, after the Victorian essayist and guru of art and architecture. Had my father been an admirer of Mr Ruskin? I did not ask him, because at that time I thought I was the *only* Ruskin. At some point during my schooldays I discovered John Ruskin's fairy story, *The King of the Golden River*, and thought it rather good. And years later, my mother was to confirm that my father had indeed named me after the Victorian writer. My other Christian name, Owen, was seldom used, and I have never really bothered with it. An extra Christian name seems quite superfluous. And besides, Owen (in Welsh) means 'brave', and I am not a brave person. I have done some foolhardy things, but more out of ignorance than bravery.

I settled down in the prep school without any fuss. Compared to the Mussoorie convent it was luxury. For lunch there was usually curry and rice (as compared to the spartan meat boiled with pumpkin, the convent speciality); for dinner there would be cutlets or a chop. There was a wartime shortage of eggs, but the school kitchen managed to make some fairly edible omelettes out of egg powder. Occasionally there were sausages, although no one could say with any certainty what was in them. On my questioning our housemaster as to their contents, he smiled mysteriously and sang the first line of a Nelson Eddy favourite—'Ah, sweet mystery of life!'

Our sausages came to be known as 'Sweet Mysteries.' This was 1943, and the end of the War was still two years away.

Flying heroes were the order of the day. There were the *Biggles* books, with a daredevil pilot as hero. And *Champion* comic books featured Rockfist Rogan of the RAF, another flying ace who, whenever he was shot down in enemy territory, took on the Nazis in the boxing ring before escaping in one of their aircraft.

Having a father in the RAF was very prestigious and I asked my father to wear his uniform whenever he came to see me. This he did, and to good effect.

'Bond's father is in the RAF,' word went round, and other boys looked at me with renewed respect. 'Does he fly bombers or fighter planes?' they asked me.

'Both,' I lied. After all, there wasn't much glamour in codes and ciphers, although they were probably just as important.

My own comic-book hero was Flying O'Flynn, an acrobatic goalkeeper who made some breathtaking saves in every issue, and kept his otherwise humble team at the top of the football league. I was soon emulating him, on our stony football field, and it wasn't long before I was the prep school goalkeeper.

Quite a few of the boys read books, the general favourites being the *William* stories, R.M. Ballantyne's adventure novels, Capt. W.E. Johns (Biggles), and any sort of spy or murder mystery. There was one boy, about my age, who was actually writing a detective story. As there was a paper shortage, he wrote in a small hand on slips of toilet paper, and stored these away in his locker. I can't remember his name, so have no idea if he grew up to become a professional writer. He left the following year, when most of the British boys began leaving India. Some had grown up in India; others had been sent out as evacuees during the Blitz.

I don't remember any special friend during the first year at the prep school, but I got on quite well with teachers and classmates. As I'd joined in mid-term, the rest of the year seemed to pass quickly. And when the Kalka-Delhi Express drew into Delhi, there was my father on the platform, wearing his uniform and looking quite spry and of course happy to see me.

He had now taken a flat in Scindia House, an apartment building facing Connaught Circus. This suited me perfectly, as it was only a few minutes from cinemas, bookshops and restaurants. Just across the road was the newly opened Milk Bar, and while my father was away at his office, I would occasionally slip out to have a milkshake—strawberry, chocolate or vanilla—and dart back home with a comic paper purchased at one of the newsstands.

All those splendid new cinemas were within easy reach too, and my father and I soon became regular cinegoers; we must have seen at least three films a week on an average. I again took to making lists of all the films I saw, including the casts as far as I could remember them. Even today, to reiterate, I can rattle off the cast of almost any Hollywood or British production of the 1940s. The films I enjoyed most that winter were *Yankee Doodle Dandy* (with James Cagney quite electric as George M. Cohan); and *This Above All*, a drama of wartime London.

When I asked my father how the film had got its title, he wrote down the lines from Shakespeare that had inspired it:

This above all, to thine own self be true,

And it must follow, as the night the day,
Thou can'st not then be false to any man.

I kept that piece of paper for many years, losing it only when I went to England.

Helping my father with his stamp collection, accompanying him to the pictures, dropping in at Wenger's for tea and muffins, bringing home a book or record—what more could a small boy of eight have asked for?

And then there were the walks.

In those days, you had only to walk a short distance to be out of New Delhi and into the surrounding fields or scrub forest. Humayun's Tomb was surrounded by a wilderness of babul and keekar trees, and so were other old tombs and monuments on the periphery of the new capital. Today they have all been swallowed up by new housing estates and government colonies, and the snarl of traffic is wonderful to behold.

New Delhi was still a small place in 1943. The big hotels (Maidens, the Swiss) were in Old Delhi. Only a few cars could be seen on the streets. Most people, including service personnel, travelled by pony-drawn tongas. When we went to the station to catch a train, we took a tonga. Otherwise we walked.

In the deserted Purana Kila my father showed me the narrow steps leading down from Humayun's library. Here the Emperor slipped and fell to his death. Not far away was Humayun's tomb. These places had few visitors then, and we could relax on the grass without being disturbed by hordes of tourists, guides, vagrants and health freaks. New Delhi still has its parks and tree-lined avenues—but

22

oh, the press of people! Who could have imagined then
that within forty years' time, the city would have
swallowed huge tracts of land way beyond Ghaziabad,
Faridabad, Gurgaon, Najafgarh, Tughlaqabad, small
towns, villages, fields, most of the Ridge and all that grew
upon it!

Change and prosperity have come to Delhi, but its
citizens are paying a high price for the privilege of living
in the capital. Too late to do anything about it now. Spread
on, great octopus—your tentacles have yet to be fully
extended.

*

If, in writing this memoir, I appear to be taking my
father's side, I suppose it is only human nature for a boy
to be loyal to the parent who stands by him, no matter
how difficult the circumstances. An eight-year-old is
bound to resent his mother's liaison with another man.
Looking back on my boyhood, I feel sure that my mother
must have had her own compulsions, her own views on
life and how it should be lived. After all, she had only been
eighteen when she had married my father, who was about
fifteen years her senior. She and her sisters had been a
fun-loving set; they enjoyed going to dances, picnics,
parties. She must have found my father too serious, too
much of a stay-at-home, happy making the morning
butter or sorting through his stamps in the evening. My
mother told me later that he was very jealous, keeping her
away from other men. And who wouldn't have been
jealous? She was young, pretty, vivacious—everyone
looked twice at her!

They were obviously incompatible. They should never have married, I suppose. In which case, of course, I would not be here, penning these memoirs.

Chapter Three

My Father's Last Letter

1944. The war dragged on. No sooner was I back in prep school than my father was transferred to Calcutta. In some ways this was a good thing because my sister Ellen was there, living with 'Calcutta Granny,' and my father could live in his own home for a change. Granny had been living on Park Lane ever since Grandfather had died.

It meant, of course, that my father couldn't come to see me in Simla during my mid-term holidays. But he wrote regularly—once a week, on an average. The War was coming to an end, peace was in the air, but there was also talk of the British leaving India as soon as the war was over. In his letters my father spoke of the preparations he was making towards that end. Obviously he saw no future for us in a free India. He was not an advocate of Empire but he took a pragmatic approach to the problems of the day. There would be a new school for me in England, he said, and meanwhile he was selling off large segments of his stamp collection so that we'd have some money to start life afresh when he left the RAF. There was also his old mother to look after, and my sister Ellen and a baby brother, William, who was to be caught in no-man's land.

I did not concern myself too much with the future. Scout camps at Tara Devi and picnics at the Brockhurst tennis courts were diversions in a round of classes, games, dormitory inspections and evening homework. We could shower in the evenings, a welcome change from the tubs of my former school; and we did not have to cover our nudity—there were no nuns in attendance, only our prefects, who were there to see that we didn't scream the place down.

Did we have sexual adventures? Of course we did. It would have been unreasonable to expect a horde of eight to twelve-year-olds to take no interest in those parts of their anatomy which were undergoing constant change during puberty. But it did not go any further than a little clandestine masturbation in the dormitories late at night. There were no scandals, no passionate affairs, at least none that I can recall. We were at the age of inquisitive and innocent enquiry; not (as yet) the age of emotional attachment or experimentation.

Sex was far down our list of priorities; far behind the exploits of the new comic-book heroes—Captain Marvel, Superman, the Green Lantern and others of their ilk. They had come into the country in the wake of the American troops, and looked like they would stay after everyone had gone. We modelled ourselves on our favourite heroes, giving each other names like Bulletman or Wonderman.

Our exploits, however, did not go far beyond the spectacular pillow-fights that erupted every now and then between the lower and upper dormitories, or one section of a dormitory and another. Those fluffy feather pillows, lovingly stitched together by fond mothers (or the darzi sitting on the verandah), would sometimes come apart, resulting in a storm of feathers sweeping across the dorm. On one occasion, the headmaster's wife, alerted by all the noise, rushed into the dorm, only to be greeted by a feather pillow full in the bosom. Mrs Priestley was a large-bosomed woman—we called her breasts 'nutcrackers'—and the pillow burst against them. She slid to the ground, buried in down. As punishment we all received the flat of her hairbrush on our posteriors. Canings were given only in the senior school.

Mrs Priestley played the piano, her husband the violin. They practised together in the assembly hall every evening. They had no children and were not particularly fond of children, as far as I could tell. In fact, Mrs Priestley had a positive antipathy for certain boys and lost no opportunity in using her brush on them. Mr Priestley showed a marked preference for upper-class English boys, of whom there were a few. He was lower middle class himself (as I discovered later).

Some good friends and companions during my two-and-a-half prep school years were Peter Blake, who did his hair in a puff like Alan Ladd; Brian Abbott, a quiet boy who boasted only of his father's hunting exploits—Abbott was a precursor to Jim Corbett, but never wrote anything; Riaz Khan, a good-natured, fun-loving boy; and Bimal Mirchandani, who grew up to become a Bombay industrialist. I don't know what happened to the others.

As I have said, I kept my father's letters, but the only one that I was able to retain (apart from some of the postcards) was the last one, which I reproduce here.

It is a good example of the sort of letter he wrote to me, and you can see why I hung on to it.

27

AA Bond 108485 (RAF)
c/o 231 Group
Rafpost
Calcutta 20/8/44

My dear Ruskin,

Thank you very much for your letter received a few days ago. I was pleased to hear that you were quite well and learning hard. We are all quite O.K. here, but I am still not strong enough to go to work after the recent attack of malaria I had. I was in hospital for a long time and that is the reason why you did not get a letter from me for several weeks.

I have now to wear glasses for reading, but I do not use them for ordinary wear—but only when I read or do book work. Ellen does not wear glasses at all now.

Do you need any new warm clothes? Your warm suits must be getting too small. I am glad to hear the rains are practically over in the hills where you are. It will be nice to have sunny days in September when your holidays are on. Do the holidays begin from the 9th of Sept? What will you do? Is there to be a Scouts Camp at Taradevi? Or will you catch butterflies on sunny days on the school Cricket Ground? I am glad to hear you have lots of friends. Next year you will be in the top class of the Prep. School. You only have 3½ months more for the Xmas holidays to come round, when you will be glad to come home, I am sure, to do more Stamp work and Library Study. The New Market is full of book shops here. Ellen loves the market.

I wanted to write before about your writing Ruskin, but forgot. Sometimes I get letters from you written in very small handwriting, as if you wanted to squeeze a lot of news into one sheet of letter paper. It is not good for you or for your eyes, to get into the habit of writing small: I know your handwriting is good and that you came 1st in class for handwriting, but try and form a larger style of writing and do not worry if you can't get all your news into one sheet of paper—but stick to big letters.

We have had a very wet month just passed. It is still cloudy, at night we have to use fans, but during the cold weather it is nice—not too cold like Delhi and not too warm either—but just moderate. Granny is quite well. She and Ellen send you their fond love. The last I heard a week ago, that William and all at Dehra were well also.

We have been without a cook for the past few days. I hope we find a good one before long. There are not many. I wish I could get our Delhi cook, the old man now famous for his 'Black Puddings' which Ellen hasn't seen since we arrived in Calcutta 4 months ago.

I have still got the Records and Gramophone and most of the best books, but as they are all getting old and some not suited to you which are only for children under 8 yrs old—I will give some to William, and Ellen and you can buy some new ones when you come home for Xmas. I am re-arranging all the stamps that became loose and topsy-turvy after people came and went through the collections to buy stamps. A good many got sold, the rest got mixed up a bit and it is now taking up all my time putting the balance of the collection in order. But as I am at home all day, unable to go to work as yet, I have lots of time to finish the work of re-arranging the Collection. Ellen loves drawing. I give her paper and a pencil and let her draw for herself without any help, to get her used to holding paper and pencil. She has got expert at using her pencil now and draws some wonderful animals like camels, elephants, dragons with many heads—cobras— rain clouds shedding buckets of water—tigers with long grass around them—horses with manes and wolves and foxes with bushy hair. Sometimes you can't see much of the animals because there is too much grass covering them or two much hair on the foxes and wolves and too much mane on the horses' necks—or too much rain from the clouds. All this decoration is made up by a sort of heavy scribbling of lines, but through it all one can see some very good shapes of animals, elephants and ostriches and other things. I will send you some.

Well, Ruskin, I hope this finds you well. With fond love from us all. Write again soon. Ever your loving daddy . . .

*

It was about two weeks after receiving this letter that I was given the news of my father's death. Those frequent bouts of malaria had undermined his health, and a severe attack of jaundice did the rest. A kind but inept teacher, Mr Murtough, was given the unenviable task of breaking the news to me. He mumbled something about God needing my father more than I did, and of course I knew what had happened and broke down and had to be taken to the infirmary, where I remained for a couple of days. It never made any sense to me why God should have needed my father more than I did, unless of course He envied my father's stamp collection. If God was Love, why did He have to break up the only loving relationship I'd known so far? What would happen to me now, I wondered . . . would I live with Calcutta Granny or some other relative

30

or be put away in an orphanage?

Mr Priestley saw me in his office and said I'd be going to my mother when school closed. He said he'd been told that I had kept my father's letters and that if I wished to put them in his safe keeping he'd see that they were not lost. I handed them over—all except the one I've reproduced here.

The day before we broke up for the school holidays, I went to Mr Priestley and asked for my letters. 'What letters?' He looked bemused, irritated. He'd had a trying day. 'My father's letters,' I told him. 'You said you'd keep them for me.' 'Did I? Don't remember. Why should I want to keep your father's letters?' 'I don't know, sir. You put them in your drawer.' He opened the drawer, shut it. 'None of your letters here. I'm very busy now, Bond. If I find any of your letters, I'll give them to you.' I was dismissed from his presence.

I never saw those letters again. And I'm glad to say I did not see Mr Priestley again. All he'd given me was a lifelong aversion to violin players.

Chapter Four

Mother and Stepfather

When I got down from the train at the Dehra Dun station—one of several boys in the 'Dehra party'—I expected to be met by my mother, or at least someone from her household. But although I waited on the platform for at least an hour, until it was emptied of passengers, porters and vendors of every description, no one who looked even remotely familiar came up to where I sat on my tin trunk, beside my bedding roll, attaché case and hockey stick. Even the platform dogs had slunk away, for I had nothing to offer them, my school sandwiches having been consumed the night before.

Other children had been met by parents and relatives and had dispersed to their homes. A junior station official came up and asked me if I was waiting for someone.

'I think so,' I said. 'I'll wait a little longer.'

A feeling of insecurity began to creep over me—a feeling that was to recur from time to time and which was to become part of my mental luggage for the rest of my life.

After another half-hour of futile waiting, I got a porter to carry my luggage out to the tonga stand—there were

32

no taxis then—and piling into one of these rickety pony-drawn contraptions, I gave the tongawallah the address of my grandmother's house on the Old Survey Road, and set off in the hope that house and grandmother still existed. It was at least three years since I had seen either.

Granny was there, of course, feeding her black pariah dog, Crazy, who recognized me, leapt on me, licked my face and then, to show his delight, ran three times around the house—a habit of his when pleased! Granny's dog had more character than any pedigreed canine in the neighbourhood.

Granny, a heavy-set, heavy-jowled woman, was a taciturn person who displayed no great joy at seeing me, but she was both surprised and concerned at my unexpected arrival in a tonga.

'Weren't you met at the station?'

'No,' I said.

'Well, they don't live here. Do you know where to go?'

'No.'

'Then I'd better come with you, I suppose.'

With great reluctance she got into the tonga. It was drawn by a white pony, and she was prejudiced against white ponies, believing them to be unruly and ill-natured. But this one got us to Dalanwala and my stepfather's rented house without mishap.

After a good deal of calling out and knocking on doors, a servant appeared and told us that the sahib and memsahib were away on a shikar trip and wouldn't be back till evening. Grandmother asked the cook-cum-bearer to prepare lunch for me and then, dismissing the tonga with the innocent white pony, hailed another

33

that was passing along the road. This one was drawn by a piebald pony. Apparently she did not feel threatened by it, or by the tongawallah, a scruffy-looking chap with yellow teeth, for she got in with some aplomb and rode off to her house, having done her duty by me. I never could fathom my maternal grandmother, or what lay behind her taciturnity. 'Calcutta Granny' I had seen only once. My maternal grandfather had died when I was just a year old. So I'd missed the companionship and attention that grandparents can often give. My father had been the best of companions, but now there was no one to take his place.

My grandmother was a strange person. She sat alone in the evenings, playing Patience, a card game which does not require another player. Her tenant, Miss Kellner, did the same thing, but she was a cripple who could not move from her chair. It never occurred to either of them to play each other at cards, though Miss Kellner did occasionally go out (in a sedan chair) to bridge parties in other European or Anglo-Indian households.

In some of my children's stories I have written about fun-loving grandfathers and doting grandmothers, but this was just wishful thinking on my part. Grandmother could be kind, but she did not *dote* on her grandchildren. If you told her you were hungry, you were presented with a slice of bread and butter. When I was really hungry, I slipped across to Miss Kellner's part of the house. She had a well-stocked larder and would ply me with cakes, scones, meringues, ginger biscuits and other delicacies.

During the school holidays, I would often go to see Miss Kellner (on the pretext of visiting Granny), and she never disappointed me.

My mother and stepfather returned from their shikar trip late at night. Before that, I'd made the acquaintance of the cook, an ayah and a baby half-brother. There was also a small garden to explore, and an orchard of guava trees. I was beginning to find that trees gave me a feeling of security, as well as privacy and a calm haven.

I should say here now that my stepfather, Mr Hari, was in no way cruel or unkind to me. He was, however, something of a playboy, who loved drinking, dancing, hunting, party-going, in other words, *la dolce vita*—and he had little or no time for a boy of ten who had just been dumped on him because there was nowhere else I could go. He did not make any attempt to relate to me and that was just as well, because he hadn't the sensitivity to make a go of being a 'father'. Even with his own children (previous and future) he led by failure rather than by example. He seemed unaware of them most of the time. Only in his later years, particularly after my mother's death, did he begin to take an interest in what we were doing.

'Calcutta Granny' died that winter, and as a result my sister Ellen also arrived, accompanied by a nanny. In her box were some of my books but none of my father's stamps. Had they *all* been sold, I wondered, and if they had, where was the money? No one seemed to know.

The nanny was sent back to Calcutta and replaced by the ayah. The household now consisted of my mother and stepfather (when they were at home), the cook-bearer, the ayah, Ellen, my baby brother William, and my baby half-brother Harold. Mr Hari's children from his first wife lived with their mother behind their shop in the town. His daughter, Premela, was one day to take over the responsibility of looking after my sister, Ellen.

From the start I insisted on having a room of my own, something I was always to insist on, even if it meant sleeping in a tin shed in the garden. My first room wasn't a tin shed; it was a nice room, with a view of the lichi trees and the road and a large open plot on the other side of the road. Dehra was then a place of open spaces and this one beckoned to me. I set out for a stroll—the first of many through the lanes and byways of this leafy little town, and the fields and tea gardens that once surrounded it.

Inevitably, one of my walks took me to. my grandmother's house. She was out that day on one of her rare visits to the Allahabad Bank, so I walked over to Miss Kellner's side of the house and found her sitting in the sun, writing letters. She was a great letter-writer, even though she held the quill pen in an awkward way, her hands being deformed.

She looked at me over her pince-nez and asked me to sit down on a *mora* beside her. She was unable to stand; her feet and hands were crippled since her early childhood in Calcutta. When she was a baby, a fond uncle had been tossing her in the air and catching her as she came down. Something had happened to distract his attention. He'd tossed her high in the air but out of reach, and she'd landed on the floor with a thud. That had been over sixty years ago. Miss Kellner's parents had died, leaving her a good income, and she had lived on, settling in Dehra Dun because of its gentler climate and restful atmosphere.

As she was unobtrusive and regular with her payments she was the ideal tenant for my grandmother. She liked having visitors, and as I have already mentioned, her larder was well stocked.

On this early visit, she invited me to play 'Snap' with her. This was a simple but rather noisy card game in which the players shouted 'Snap!' whenever they put down cards that matched. I forget the other rules and I never became a card-player, but Miss Kellner and I enjoyed ourselves hugely for half an hour, at the end of which time she plied me with cakes and meringues.

I'd found a friend at last, and decided I'd be one of her regular visitors.

Another elderly person who befriended me was Dhuki, my grandmother's gardener. He was always down on his haunches, weeding the flower beds, and I could talk to him without looking up, as a child must do when talking to an upright adult. I'd ask Dhuki the names of different flowers and of course he knew them all, although he preferred to use the Hindustani 'gulab' for rose and 'genda' for marigold. Otherwise he'd use most of the English names—phlox, zinnia, gerbera, sweet-pea, geranium. Grandmother did not care for the smell of marigolds and tossed them out, but Miss Kellner allowed them to flourish on her side of the house—she said they kept the mosquitoes away!

Dhuki was a skinny, spindle-legged forty-year-old who looked sixty. He and his wife (who was sometimes heard but seldom seen) had been producing a baby a year for quite some time, and there were about twelve survivors ranging in age from six months to sixteen years. They could be seen playing in the guava orchard behind the bungalow and Dhuki did not encourage them to venture into the front garden.

I seemed to get on with old or elderly people, and at this point in my life had no desire to make young friends.

I began to read whatever books came my way. As very few did, I could not be choosy. But whatever they were—cheap thriller or Victorian classic or even erotica (there was some of that around too)—it provided me with an escape from the reality of my situation. And it was during those first winter holidays in Dehra that I became a bookworm and, ultimately, a book lover and writer in embryo.

*

When my mother and Mr Hari went off on their two or three-day shikar trips, I was usually left at home; but on one or two occasions they took me along, hoping perhaps to instil in me a love for big-game hunting!

I have described one of these jaunts before, in a story, *Copperfield in the Jungle*, so I will just summarize it by saying that my boredom and ennui were relieved by the discovery of a bookshelf in the Forest Rest House where we were staying. And while the great hunters were dashing off into the jungle with their guns (and frequently coming back empty-handed), I discovered several authors who were to give me considerable pleasure then and in the years to come: M.R. James (*Ghost Stories of An Antiquary*), P.G. Wodehouse (*Love among the Chickens* was my introduction to PGW), and A.A. Milne (with *The Red House Mystery*). I was always to prefer Milne's adult stories and plays to his children's stories. (I think he did, too, in the end.) Toy animals voicing human sentiments never did fascinate me. Appealing though animals may be as pets or in the wild, their civilization is different from ours. A better one, possibly; but distinct from ours. The only time I found an animal take an interest in a book was when, quite recently, a monkey got into my Mussoorie home and tore several of my manuscripts to shreds. Some might say that he was only doing what I should have done myself, but even my worst critics haven't gone that far. I like animals but I refuse to be sentimental about them.

Back in the 1940s, even though the visual media was restricted to the cinema, books were scarce commodities in small-town India. Anyone who was hooked on reading had to go in search of books.

Poking around in the back verandah of Granny's house on Old Survey Road, I found a number of books, obviously untouched for years, tucked away in a chest of drawers. I had never seen my grandmother read anything apart from letters, so they could not have been hers. The name 'E. Sims' was inscribed in some of them, and I learnt later that she was probably a great-aunt who had died some years previously.

A few of the books were religious tracts, obviously unsuitable for an enquiring mind, but several Victorian novelists were included in the small collection, and there were two or three novels by Dickens. I picked up *Nicholas Nickleby* and carried it back to my stepfather's rented house in Dalanwala.

A fortnight later I was back in Granny's back verandah, and this time I came up with a book of stories about South Africa, *The Little Karoo* by Pauline Smith, and *The Virginian* by Owen Wister, a novel that was a precursor of the modern 'Western'. Both books had 'E. Sims' on the flyleaf, and it was clear that her tastes were nothing if not eclectic.

I never could find out much about 'E. Sims,' other than

that she was a distant relative, but she certainly played a formative role in my development as a reader (and possibly as a writer), because I devoured almost all the books in that small collection (including such diverse works as *Little Women* and *The Invisible Man*) and to this day remain ready to read almost anything provided it has tone, style and substance.

Chapter Five

Dehra Dun—Winter of '45

It snowed in Dehra that winter—on the evening of the 2nd of January, the day after another baby half-brother was born.

Normally it did not snow in Dehra. You had to look up to the Mussoorie range, to see the white-crested peaks after the first snowfall. For it to snow in the valley was quite freakish.

It came down quite suddenly, while I was returning from one of my walks. Soon the lichi and guava trees were covered with a soft mantle of snow. Dehra had never looked prettier—I ran indoors to tell my mother. She was in bed with the baby.

'It's snowing outside, Mum!' I cried excitedly.

'I don't feel like joking just now, Ruskin,' she said. 'I'm very tired.'

So I ran outside, plucked a snow-covered twig off one of the lichi trees and took it inside to show my mother. She looked pleased and brightened up considerably.

Next morning there was lots of snow lying around, and I played snowballs with my stepfather's mechanic and some of the neighbourhood boys. Then the sun came out, and by noon the snow had vanished.

The following day I went to see Miss Kellner. She told me that it had snowed in Dehra forty years earlier, when she had first arrived in the town. Now perhaps it was a sign that she should go away.

'Don't go,' I said. 'Wait for the next snowfall.'

So we played 'Snap' and I finished all her ginger biscuits.

Then she was carried indoors for her bath. As she couldn't stand up, or even straighten up, she had to be bathed by her ayah. But she never missed her daily bath; it had become a sort of ritual with her.

She had her own personal rickshaw and four liveried men to pull it. As she couldn't climb into tongas or cars, she had to use the rickshaw. She was only a featherweight and the rickshawmen flew down the road with her; I couldn't keep up with them. She enjoyed these rides and took one every evening. The rickshaw was painted sky blue.

Her parents had left her a fair amount of money; otherwise she could not have afforded these luxuries. And she could not have survived without them. But her mind was far from being crippled. She possessed all her faculties—which was more than could be said for many who had the use of all their limbs.

During the War years Dehra was a lively little town. It had been made a recreational centre for war-weary Allied troops, and there were large contingents of British and American solders stationed on the outskirts. As a result, cafés, dance-halls, bars and even a couple of 'nightclubs' sprang up all over the place, and the subsequent revelry continued until the early hours of each morning.

My mother and Mr Hari went out almost every night.
The old Ford convertible would bring them back at two or
three in the morning. My insecurity was such that I would
often wonder how I would cope if they had a fatal accident
coming home, or if some avenging tigress got her own back
in the jungle. Would I have to look after my sister, baby
brother and two half-brothers? And where would the
money come from?

Money did not seem to be a concern with my mother
and stepfather. There seemed to be plenty of it around and
I presumed Mr Hari's motor workshop was flourishing.

But my instincts were sound and my fears not without
foundation; for I returned from one of my afternoon walks
to find all our boxes, bedding, furniture, pots and pans,
out on the driveway. Apparently there were several
months' arrears of rent due to the landlord, and he had
secured an eviction order.

We ended up in Granny's house—poor soul, she was
much put out, her cherished privacy shattered by her
youngest daughter's unconventional lifestyle—and
stayed there for the remainder of my winter holidays.

*

Spring came to the foothills in February, and Dehra's
gardens were at their best then. Masses of sweet peas
filled the air with their delicious scent; bright yellow
California poppies formed a carpet of their own; scarlet
poinsettias greeted each other over hedges and garden
walls; snapdragons of many hues gave off their own
elusive scent; bright red poppies danced in the slightest
breeze. Those were the days when houses and bungalows

had spacious compounds, with space for flower and vegetable gardens and even orchards. Over the years the pressures of population and the demand for more living space has meant the disappearance of large gardens. Some of the old bungalows survive in the middle of cramped housing estates, and there is little room left for flowers and fruit trees except up at Rajpur or parts of Dalanwala.

Miss Kellner told me that Granny's sweet peas used to win prizes at the annual flower show (held every year in the first week of March), but after Grandfather's death (when I was just two), she seldom exhibited her flowers. Dhuki, who had been with her many years, continued to look after the garden.

Miss Kellner did not take much interest in the garden but her little sitting room was crowded with bric-a-brac: ornate vases, decorative wall-plates, china figurines, little wooden toys . . . It was impossible to move around without knocking something over, so her visitors wisely stuck to her dining room or verandah or, better still, sat out beside her under the pomalo tree, while she shuffled her cards or did her hisaab (the day's accounts) or scribbled notes to her friends.

All this was a far cry from the feverish nightlife of the 'Casino' or the 'White House' or 'Green's,' where roistering soldiers on leave gathered late in the evenings to dance with the few Anglo-Indian girls who still lived in Dehra and were looking for a little fun and maybe even romance. These dances often ended in drunken brawls, sometimes between British and American servicemen. The latter were better paid and free with their money, and this led to some resentment.

One of these girls, a pretty little thing called Doreen, had fussed over me whenever my mother had taken me to the store below the Casino, where she worked. She must have been eighteen or nineteen. I couldn't help noticing that she had lovely legs and full sensuous lips that I longed to kiss.

One evening she invited me to accompany her to a dance up at the Casino, and my mother and stepfather making no objection, I escorted her into the restaurant-cum-ballroom where the local band was playing the latest Glenn Miller hits. The hall was full of tobacco smoke and beer fumes. Doreen gave me a glass of rum, which I downed without any hesitation. I then led her on to the dance floor, much to everyone's delight. An eleven-year-old doing the foxtrot with one of the town beauties must have been a sight to behold. Unfortunately, the next dance went to one of the 'Tommies' (soldiers), and soon she was bestowing her favours on the entire contingent of Allied troops in the dance hall while I moodily played with a plate of fish fingers that had been placed in front of me.

However, came the midnight hour—it was New Year's Eve—and the lights went off, and while everyone sang 'Auld Lang Syne,' Doreen gathered me in her perfumed arms and planted a long sweet kiss on my hungry lips.

It was my first real kiss and I savour it still.

*

I heard later that Doreen married one of her soldier boys and went to live in one of London's working-class districts.

The exodus of British and Anglo-Indian families was beginning even as the War ended. For some the choice was a hard one. They had no prospects in England, no relatives there. And they had no prospects in India unless they were very well qualified. For many Anglo-Indians and 'poor whites,' assisted passages to England were the order of the day. By the time 1947, the year of Indian Independence, came around, most of these people had gone, to make some sort of living in the U.K. The rush to Australia took place much later.

I suppose I qualified as a 'poor white.' But there were many whose circumstances were much worse than mine.

Take Mrs Deeds and her seventeen-year-old son, Howard.

I met them in the winter of '45-'46, at which time my mother was managing the Green's Hotel (it has long since vanished) just off Rajpur Road. My stepfather's showroom and garage had closed down (for the second time) and he was once again living with his first wife, who now ran her own grocery store. My mother had taken a manager's job, running the Green's Hotel, which had seen better days. Her modest salary helped to keep us all going, although, fortunately, my school fees were being paid by the RAF, which also sent an allowance for my sister.

The Green's was a well-laid out bungalow-type hotel with about twenty rooms, but in those days it was rare for more than two or three of them to be occupied. The post-War slump had already hit Dehra. This lean period was to continue into the early fifties.

My mother had allowed me to occupy one of the small single rooms at the back of the hotel for the duration of my holidays. Occupying the next room was Mrs Deeds, in her late thirties, and her teenager son, with all their possessions. God knows where they had come from, or why they had come to Dehra. They had no friends or relatives in the town. They were the flotsam of Empire, jettisoned by the very people who had brought them into existence. There were many such down-and-outs.

A good-looking woman was Mrs Deeds, but an alcoholic. When she was hitting the bottle, her son ridiculed her, and they had the most terrible fights. He was a self-righteous youth who blamed his mother for the situation they were in—without support (for she had been deserted by her husband), without a home (for that had been sold for a song), and without any prospects (for there was no one to turn to). Her feeling of guilt was compounded by her son's attacks on her, and as a result she hit the bottle with renewed vigour.

When she was broke, she would cadge a drink from my mother. When he was broke, he would borrow the odd rupee from me.

She could not pay her bills at Green's and had to leave. They took up residence in the second-class waiting room at the railway station. An indulgent stationmaster allowed them to stay there for several weeks; then they moved into a cheap, seedy little hotel outside the station.

Mrs Deeds, like Mr Micawber, was always expecting a 'remittance' from the man who'd bought her property in Naini Tal but had yet to pay the main amount. She'd sold her wedding ring and gold watch to pay for drink and the rent. Howard loafed around, talking big. When they got to England or Australia or wherever they were going, he'd find a job to his liking. It did not occur to him to look for one in Dehra.

Late one evening, after Mrs Deeds had been drinking at a small liquor shop near the clock tower, she set out to cross the maidan to see someone at the club who had promised her some help. She was set upon by a gang of three or four young men who beat her badly and then raped her. Although she cried out for help, no one came to her assistance. The maidan had always been a safe place; but times were changing.

My mother went to see her and gave her what help she could. Then the remittance (or part of it) arrived, and Mrs Deeds and her son went their way and presumably started a new life abroad.

*

I went to see Miss Kellner.

There she was, hunched up in her garden chair, making the most of her restricted life—broken nose, twisted hands, shattered feet—scribbling little notes to her friends and then inviting me to a game of 'Snap'.

No one was going to rape Miss Kellner.

Or, for that matter, Mrs Kennedy, another piece of human flotsam, now in her sixties and engaged by my mother to look after Ellen.

Mrs Kennedy was a widow, Irish as her name suggests. Unlike Mrs Deeds, she had fond memories of her husband, who had died when quite a young man. He was a beautiful singer, according to Mrs Kennedy; sang everything from opera to Irish ballads. She gave me her own rendering of 'Danny Boy' in a warbling contralto but lost the melody half-way through and ended on a cracked note.

'Did you sing duets?' I asked.

'No, he preferred singing alone.'

I wasn't surprised but refrained from saying so.

'He was a tenor—sang like John McCormack,' she told me.

Personally, I preferred a robust baritone like Nelson Eddy or Laurence Tibbett, but to please her I went through an album of old records and found one of McCormack singing 'When Irish Eyes are Smiling.' We discovered a small wind-up gramophone in one of the hotel rooms, and she took it to her room and played the record over and over again.

She was tall and angular and I don't think she could ever have been good-looking, but I enjoyed listening to her. Older people have always found me a patient and sympathetic listener. Sometimes they are inclined to ramble on, but if you listen carefully, you will often find that they have some interesting tales to tell.

But my sister Ellen took a strong dislike to Mrs Kennedy, as indeed she did to anyone who was put in charge of her. A backward child with defects of vision and the first signs of epilepsy, she had very strong likes and dislikes. For instance, she hated bananas, and if Mrs Kennedy tried to reason with her by saying, 'Bananas are good for you, dear,' bananas would fly about the room and everyone present would have to duck for cover.

Anything that was 'Good for her' was immediately resented and cast aside. Ellen longed to be a bad girl, but she was to retain for all her life the mind of a six-year-old.

'Brain cutlets,' I informed her one day as this delicacy arrived on the dining table. 'Bad for you. You're not supposed to eat them.'

She immediately devoured three brain cutlets and asked for more. To this day she loves brain cutlets, under the impression that they will make her very wicked.

Mrs Kennedy, however, decided to leave us the day she received a grapefruit in her eye. Ellen did not see straight, and on this occasion she was really aiming at me (I had been teasing her); but the grapefruit, thrown with considerable force, struck Mrs Kennedy instead.

She went to work as a dormitory matron in a local convent school, and as a parting present I gave her the John McCormack record.

Chapter Six

The Playing Fields of Simla

It had been a lonely winter for a twelve-year-old boy.

I hadn't really got over my father's untimely death two years previously; nor had I as yet reconciled myself to my mother's marriage to the Punjabi gentleman who dealt in second-hand cars. The three-month winter break over, I was almost happy to return to my boarding school in Simla—that elegant hill station once celebrated by Kipling and soon to lose its status as the summer capital of the Raj in India.

It wasn't as though I had many friends at school. I had always been a bit of a loner, shy and reserved, looking out only for my father's rare visits—on his brief leaves from RAF duties—and to my sharing his tent or Air Force hutment outside Delhi or Karachi. Those unsettled but happy days would not come again. I needed a friend but it was not easy to find one among a horde of rowdy, pea-shooting fourth formers, who carved their names on desks and stuck chewing gum on the class teacher's chair. Had I grown up with other children, I might have developed a taste for schoolboy anarchy; but, in sharing my father's loneliness after his separation from my

51

mother, I had turned into a premature adult. The mixed nature of my reading—Dickens, Richmal Crompton, Tagore and *Champion* and *Film Fun* comics—probably reflected the confused state of my life. A book reader was rare even in those pre-electronic times. On rainy days most boys played cards or Monopoly, or listened to Artie Shaw on the wind-up gramophone in the common room.

After a month in the fourth form I began to notice a new boy, Omar, and then only because he was a quiet, almost taciturn person who took no part in the form's feverish attempts to imitate the Marx Brothers at the circus. He showed no resentment at the prevailing anarchy: nor did he make a move to participate in it. Once he caught me looking at him, and he smiled ruefully, tolerantly. Did I sense another adult in the class? Someone who was a little older than his years?

Even before we began talking to each other, Omar and I developed an understanding of sorts, and we'd nod almost respectfully to each other when we met in the classroom corridors or the environs of dining hall or dormitory. We were not in the same house. The house system practised its own form of apartheid, whereby a member of, say, Curzon House was not expected to fraternize with someone belonging to Rivaz or Lefroy! Those public schools certainly knew how to clamp you into compartments. However, these barriers vanished when Omar and I found ourselves selected for the School Colts' hockey team—Omar as a full-back, I as goalkeeper. I think a defensive position suited me by nature. In all modesty I have to say that I made a good goalkeeper, both at hockey and football. And fifty years on, I am still keeping goal. Then I did it between goalposts, now I do it off the field—protecting a family, protecting my independence as a writer. . .

The taciturn Omar now spoke to me occasionally, and we combined well on the field of play. A good understanding is needed between goalkeeper and full-back. We were on the same wavelength. I anticipated his moves, he was familiar with mine. Years later, when I read Conrad's *The Secret Sharer*, I thought of Omar.

It wasn't until we were away from the confines of school, classroom and dining hall that our friendship flourished. The hockey team travelled to Sanawar on the next mountain range, where we were to play a couple of matches against our old rivals, the Lawrence Royal Military School. This had been my father's old school, but I did not know that in his time it had also been a military orphanage. Grandfather, who had been a private foot soldier—of the likes of Kipling's Mulvaney, Otheris and Learoyd—had joined the Scottish Rifles after leaving home at the age of seventeen. He had died while his children were still very young, but my father's more rounded education had enabled him to become an officer.

Omar and I were thrown together a good deal during the visit to Sanawar, and in our more leisurely moments, strolling undisturbed around a school where we were guests and not pupils, we exchanged life histories and other confidences. Omar, too, had lost his father,—had I sensed that before?—shot in some tribal encounter on the Frontier, for he hailed from the lawless lands beyond Peshawar. A wealthy uncle was seeing to Omar's education. The RAF was now seeing to mine.

We wandered into the school chapel, and there I found my father's name—A.A. Bond—on the school's roll of honour board: old boys who had lost their lives while serving during the two World Wars.

'What did his initials stand for?' asked Omar.

'Aubrey Alexander.'

'Unusual names, like yours. Why did your parents call you Ruskin?'

'I am not sure. I think my father liked the works of John Ruskin, who wrote on serious subjects like art and architecture. I don't think anyone reads him now. They'll read *me*, though!' I had already started writing my first book. It was called *Nine Months* (the length of the school term, not a pregnancy), and it described some of the happenings at school and lampooned a few of our teachers. I had filled three slim exercise books with this premature literary project, and I allowed Omar to go through them. He must have been my first reader and critic. 'They're very interesting,' he said, 'but you'll get into trouble if someone finds them. Especially Mr Oliver.' And he read out an offending verse—

Olly, Olly, Olly, with his balls on a trolley,
And his arse all painted green!

I have to admit it wasn't great literature. I was better at hockey and football. I made some spectacular saves, and we won our matches against Sanawar. When we returned to Simla, we were school heroes for a couple of days and lost some of our reticence; we were even a little more forthcoming with other boys. And then Mr Fisher, my housemaster, discovered my literary opus, *Nine Months*, under my mattress, and took it away and read it (as he told me later) from cover to cover. Corporal

54

punishment then being in vogue, I was given six of the best with a springy malacca cane, and my manuscript was torn up and deposited in Fisher's waste-paper basket. All I had to show for my efforts were some purple welts on my bottom. These were proudly displayed to all who were interested, and I was a hero for another two days.

'Will you go away too when the British leave India?' Omar asked me one day.

'I don't think so,' I said. 'My stepfather is Indian.'

'Everyone is saying that our leaders and the British are going to divide the country. Simla will be in India, Peshawar in Pakistan!'

'Oh, it won't happen,' I said glibly. 'How can they cut up such a big country?' But even as we chatted about the possibility, Nehru and Jinnah and Mountbatten and all those who mattered were preparing their instruments for major surgery.

Before their decision impinged on our lives and everyone else's, we found a little freedom of our own—in an underground tunnel that we discovered below the third flat.

It was really part of an old, disused drainage system, and when Omar and I began exploring it, we had no idea just how far it extended. After crawling along on our bellies for some twenty feet, we found ourselves in complete darkness. Omar had brought along a small pencil torch, and with its help we continued writhing forward (moving backwards would have been quite impossible) until we saw a glimmer of light at the end of the tunnel. Dusty, musty, very scruffy, we emerged at last on to a grassy knoll, a little way outside the school boundary.

It's always a great thrill to escape beyond the boundaries that adults have devised. Here we were in unknown territory. To travel without passports—that would be the ultimate in freedom!

But more passports were on their way—and more boundaries.

Lord Mountbatten, viceroy and governor-general-to-be, came for our Founder's Day and gave away the prizes. I had won a prize for something or the other, and mounted the rostrum to receive my book from this towering, handsome man in his pinstripe suit. Bishop Cotton's was then the premier school of India, often referred to as the 'Eton of the East'. Viceroys and governors had graced its functions. Many of its boys had gone on to eminence in the civil services and armed forces. There was one 'old boy' about whom they maintained a stolid silence—General Dyer, who had ordered the massacre at Amritsar and destroyed the trust that had been building up between Britain and India.

Now Mountbatten spoke of the momentous events that were happening all around us—the War had just come to an end, the United Nations held out the promise of a world living in peace and harmony, and India, an equal partner with Britain, would be among the great nations. . .

A few weeks later, Bengal and Punjab provinces were bisected. Riots flared up across northern India, and there was a great exodus of people crossing the newly drawn frontiers of Pakistan and India. Homes were destroyed, thousands lost their lives.

The common-room radio and the occasional newspaper kept us abreast of events, but in our tunnel Omar and I felt immune from all that was happening, worlds away from all the pillage, murder and revenge. And outside the tunnel, on the pine knoll below the school, there was fresh untrodden grass, sprinkled with clover and daisies, the only sounds the hammering of a woodpecker, the distant insistent call of the Himalayan barbet. Who could touch us there?

'And when all the wars are done,' I said, 'a butterfly will still be beautiful.'

'Did you read that somewhere?'

'No, it just came into my head.'

'Already you're a writer.'

'No, I want to play hockey for India or football for Arsenal. Only winning teams!'

'You can't win forever. Better to be a writer.'

When the monsoon rains arrived, the tunnel was flooded, the drain choked with rubble. We were allowed out to the cinema, to see Lawrence Olivier's *Hamlet*, a film that did nothing to raise our spirits on a wet and gloomy afternoon—but it was our last picture that year, because communal riots suddenly broke out in Simla's Lower Bazaar, an area that was still much as Kipling had described it— 'a man who knows his way there can defy all the police of India's summer capital'—and we were confined to school indefinitely.

One morning after chapel, the headmaster announced that the Muslim boys—those who had their homes in what was now Pakistan—would have to be evacuated, sent to their homes across the border with an armed convoy.

The tunnel no longer provided an escape for us. The bazaar was out of bounds. The flooded playing field was deserted. Omar and I sat on a damp wooden bench and talked about the future in vaguely hopeful terms; but we didn't solve any problems. Mountbatten and Nehru and Jinnah were doing all the solving.

It was soon time for Omar to leave—he along with some fifty other boys from Lahore, Pindi and Peshawar. The rest of us—Hindus, Christians, Parsis—helped them load their luggage into the waiting trucks. A couple of boys broke down and wept. So did our departing school captain, a Pathan who had been known for his stoic and unemotional demeanour. Omar waved cheerfully to me and I waved back. We had vowed to meet again some day.

The convoy got through safely enough. There was only one casualty—the school cook, who had strayed into an off-limits area in the foothills town of Kalka and been set upon by a mob. He wasn't seen again.

Towards the end of the school year, just as we were all getting ready to leave for the school holidays, I received a letter from Omar. He told me something about his new school and how he missed my company and our games and our tunnel to freedom. I replied and gave him my home address, but I did not hear from him again. The land, though divided, was still a big one, and we were very small.

Some seventeen or eighteen years later I did get news of Omar, but in an entirely different context. India and Pakistan were at war and in a bombing raid over Ambala, not far from Simla, a Pakistani plane was shot down. Its crew died in the crash. One of them, I learnt later, was Omar.

Did he, I wonder, get a glimpse of the playing fields we knew so well as boys?

Perhaps memories of his schooldays flooded back as he flew over the foothills. Perhaps he remembered the tunnel through which we were able to make our little escape to freedom.

But there are no tunnels in the sky.

Chapter Seven

Reading was My Religion

In January 1948, Mahatma Gandhi was assassinated.

I had gone to the pictures at one of Dehra's new cinemas—'The Hollywood' on Chakrata Road—and the film was called *Blossoms in the Dust*; but it had been showing for about ten minutes when the projector stopped running. The lights came on and the manager appeared at one of the doors to announce that news had just been received that Gandhiji, father of the nation, had been shot dead. The cinema would be closed for a week. We were given our money back.

I walked disconsolately home across the maidan, shocked by the event and also a little dismayed that I wouldn't be able to see another picture for at least a week. (And I never did see *Blossoms* in its entirety.) As I was only thirteen at the time, I don't think I could be accused of a lack of sensitivity. As I walked across the vast maidan—it was now late evening—I passed little groups of people talking about what had happened and how it might affect the course of politics in the country. The assassin belonged to the majority community, and there was undisguised relief that the tragedy would not result in more communal riots. Gandhiji had already become history. Now he was to achieve sainthood.

Oddly enough my sister Ellen took it to heart more than anyone else in the family. She would spend hours drawing pictures of Gandhi. As her eyesight was poor, some of these portraits took weird shapes, but sometimes you could recognize the great man's glasses, chappals and walking stick.

We had moved again. My stepfather was supporting my mother once more, so she had given up the job at Green's, which was about to close down. They had rented a small, rather damp bungalow on the Eastern Canal Road, and I had a dark little room which leaked at several places when it rained. On wet winter nights it had a rather spooky atmosphere; the drip of water, the scurrying of rats in the space between the ceiling and corrugated tin roof, and the nightly visitation of a small bat which got in through a gap in the wall and swooped around the room, snapping up moths. I would stay up into the early hours reading *Oliver Twist* (pinched from Granny's house), *Wuthering Heights* (all in one sitting, during a particularly stormy night) and *Shakespeare's Complete Works*—a lofty volume of Shakespeare's plays and poems, which, till then, was the only book in the house that I hadn't read. The print was very small but I set myself the task of reading right through, and achieved this feat during the winter holidays. Of the plays I enjoyed *The Tempest* more than any other. Of the longer poems *The Rape of Lucrece* was the most intriguing but I found it difficult to reconcile its authorship with that of the plays. They were so robust; the poems formalized, watery by comparison.

I realize now that my mother was a brave woman. She stuck it out with Mr Hari who, as a businessman, was a complete disaster. He'd lost on his photographic saloon, which had now been sold by his first wife; he had lost on his motor workshop and he had lost his car sales agencies. He was up against large income tax arrears and he was irregular with all his payments. But he was popular with his workmen and mechanics, as he was quite happy to sit and drink with them, or take them along on his shikar expeditions. In this way everyone had a good time, even though his customers grew more irate by the day. Repair jobs were seldom finished on time. If a customer left a decent looking car with him for servicing, my stepfather would use it for two or three months, on the pretext of 'testing' it, before handing it back to the owner.

But his heart was in the right place. During the communal riots of '47, he, a Hindu, was instrumental in saving a number of Muslim lives, driving friends or employees to safer locations, or even upto the Pakistan border.

He never had a harsh word for me. Sometimes I wish he had!

*

The RAF had undertaken to pay for my schooling, so I was able to continue at BCS.

Back in Simla I found a sympathetic soul in Mr Jones, an ex-Army Welshman who taught us divinity. He did not have the qualifications to teach us anything else, but I think I learnt more from him than from most of our more qualified staff. He had even got me to read the Bible (King

James version) for the classical simplicity of its style.

Mr Jones got on well with small boys, one reason being that he never punished them. Alone among the philistines he was the only teacher to stand out against corporal punishment. He waged a lone campaign against the custom of caning boys for their misdemeanours, and in this respect was far ahead of his time. The other masters thought him a little eccentric, and he lost his seniority because of his refusal to administer physical punishment.

But there was nothing eccentric about Mr Jones, unless it was the pet pigeon that followed him everywhere and sometimes perched on his bald head. He managed to keep the pigeon (and his cigar) out of the classroom, but his crowded, untidy bachelor quarters reeked of cigar smoke.

He had a passion for the works of Dickens, and when he discovered that I had read *Nickleby* and *Sketches by Boz*, he allowed me to look at his set of the *Complete Works*, with the illustrations by Phiz. I launched into *David Copperfield*, which I thoroughly enjoyed, identifying myself with young David, his triumphs and tribulations. After reading *Copperfield* I decided it was a fine thing to be a writer. The seed had already been sown, and although in my imagination I still saw myself as an Arsenal goalkeeper or a Gene Kelly-type tap-dancer, I think I knew in my heart that I was best suited to the written word. I was topping the class in essay writing, although I had an aversion to studying the texts that were prescribed for Eng. lit. classes.

Mr Jones, with his socialist, Dickensian viewpoint, had an aversion for P.G. Wodehouse, whose comic novels I greatly enjoyed. He told me that these novels glamorized the most decadent aspects of upper class English life (which was probably true), and that only recently, during the War (when he was interned in France), Wodehouse had been making propaganda broadcasts on behalf of Germany. This was true, too; although years later when I read the texts of those broadcasts (in *Performing Flea*), they seemed harmless enough.

But Mr Jones did have a point—Wodehouse was hopelessly out of date, for when I went to England after leaving school, I couldn't find anyone remotely resembling a Wodehouse character. Except perhaps Ukridge, who was always borrowing money from his friends in order to set up in some business or the other; he was universal.

The school library—the Anderson Library—was fairly well stocked, and it was to be something of a haven for me over the next three years. There were always writers, past or present, to 'discover'—and I still have a tendency to ferret out writers who have been ignored, neglected or forgotten.

After *Copperfield* the novel that most influenced me was Hugh Walpole's *Fortitude*, an epic account of another young writer in the making. Its opening line still acts as a clarion call when I feel depressed or as though I am getting nowhere: 'Tisn't life that matters, but the courage you bring to it.'

Walpole's more ambitious works have been forgotten, but his stories and novels of the macabre are still worth reading—*Mr Perrin and Mr Trail, Portrait of a Man with Red Hair, The White Tower* . . . And, of course, *Fortitude*. I returned to it last year and found it was still stirring stuff.

But life wasn't all books. At the age of fifteen I was at

my best as a football goalkeeper, hockey player, athlete. I was also acting in school plays and taking part in debates. I wasn't much of a boxer—a sport I disliked—but I had learnt to use my head to good effect, and managed to get myself disqualified by butting the other fellow in the head or midriff. As all games were compulsory, I had to overcome my fear of water and learn to swim a little. Mr Jones taught me to do the breast stroke, saying it was more suited to my temperament than the splash and dash stuff.

The only thing I couldn't do was sing, and although I loved listening to great singers, from Caruso to Gigli, I couldn't sing a note. Our music teacher, Mrs Knight, put me in the school choir because, she said, I *looked* like a choir boy, all pink and shining in a cassock and surplice, but she forbade me from actually singing. I was to open my mouth with the others, but on no account was I to allow any sound to issue from it.

This took me back to the convent in Mussoorie where I had been given piano lessons, probably at my father's behest. The nun who was teaching me would get so exasperated with my stubborn inability to strike the right chord or play the right notes that she would crack me over the knuckles with a ruler—thus effectively putting an end to any interest I might have had in learning to play a musical instrument. Mr Priestley's violin, in the prep school, and now Mrs Knight's organ-playing, were none too inspiring.

Insensitive though I may have been to high notes and low notes, diminuendos and crescendos, I was nevertheless sensitive to sound—birdsong, the hum of the breeze playing in tall trees, the rustle of autumn leaves, crickets chirping, water splashing and murmuring in brooks, the sea sighing on the sand—all natural sounds, indicating a certain harmony in the natural world.

Man-made sounds—the roar of planes, the blare of horns, the thunder of trucks and engines, the baying of a crowd—are usually ugly. But some gifted humans have tried to rise above it by creating great music; and we must not scorn the also-rans, those who come down hard on their organ pedals, or emulate cicadas with their violin playing.

Although I was quite popular at Bishop Cotton's, after Omar's departure I did not have many close friends. There was, of course, young A——, my junior by two years, who followed me everywhere until I gave in and took him to the pictures in town, or fed him at the tuck shop.

There were just one or two boys who actually read books for pleasure. We tend to think of that era as one when there were no distractions such as television, computer games and the like. But reading has always been a minority pastime. People say children don't read any more. This may be true of the vast majority, but I know many boys and girls who enjoy reading; far more than I encountered when I was a schoolboy. In those days there were comics and the radio and the cinema. I went to the cinema whenever I could, but that did not keep me from reading almost everything that came my way. And so it is today. Book readers are special people, and they will always turn to books as the ultimate pleasure. Those who do not read are the unfortunate ones. There's nothing wrong with them; but they are missing out on one of life's compensations and rewards. A great book is a friend that never lets you down. You can return to it again and again, and the joy first derived from it will still be there.

I think it is fair to say that when I was a boy, reading was my true religion. It helped me to discover my soul.

Chapter Eight

A Walking Person

Stilboestrol!

Now there's a name to conjure up memories, but not very fond or romantic ones . . .

At the age of fifteen I was grievously afflicted with acne. Horrible pimples covered my face, back, neck and shoulders. Soaps, lotions and creams proved useless at clearing up the condition. Finally my housemaster sent me to the school doctor, one of those know-alls who were only too eager to prescribe the latest drugs on the market. Looking me over he had come to the decision (why, I've no idea) that my acne was due to an excess of male hormones and what I needed was a course of pills containing female hormones!

Well, the pimples remained but other things started happening. Within a few weeks of starting the treatment I found that the nipples on my chest were slightly enlarged! I was slowing down, my physical responses were not as sharp as they used to be; from being first or second on the athletics track, I was now bringing up the rear of the field. And my goalkeeping skills were not what they had been—I was letting the ball get past me with increasing frequency.

'What's wrong with you, Bond?' asked my housemaster, Mr Fisher, impatiently. 'Have you been indulging in solitary sex?'

If only I had, I might have been in better shape. But when I went to the doctor again, still covered in pimples, all he could do was prescribe another bottle of Stilboestrol tablets. By the end of the term, losing my place in goal, unable to complete the three-mile 'marathon', and finding some disturbing changes taking place in my body, I finally put two and two together and came to the conclusion that the tablets were the cause of my problems. This suspicion was reinforced by an article on hormones that I read in *Life* magazine. I threw the remaining tablets away. The damage had been done but not completely, and I was to recover some of my old skills in the following year.

The acne remained with me for another year, and finally disappeared of its own accord. I think the discovery of 'solitary sex' helped. Certainly, I have a better complexion at sixty-three than I had when I was sixteen.

*

That was the era of the wonder drugs. Penicillin had only just started being used as a miracle cure for gangrene from wounds, pneumonia, the venereal diseases and other previously fatal infections, and in time to come I was to be grateful for the discovery of penicillin and some of the other antibiotics. But the administration of male or female hormones for various physical problems seemed questionable. Even today, almost fifty years later, they can be a risky business. I wonder what got into that 'progressive' doctor's head to make him experiment on me? Treat the patient by all means, but don't play games with his biological make-up.

I received better advice from Bansi, the tonga driver who befriended me during my next winter holiday in Dehra.

'You must get rid of all that semen you've got stored away,' he said. In other words, solitary sex!

And he was right. The pimples soon vanished. I wished I'd discovered his remedy sooner.

At that time it was difficult for me to make friends of my own age. I was shy by nature and there were few if any families with whom my mother was on visiting terms. She had come in for a certain amount of social ostracism, particularly from the better-off Anglo-Indians and domiciled Europeans who disapproved of everything she had done. Nor did my stepfather have any good social connections outside his business circle. And so it wasn't surprising that some of my companions and familiars belonged to the servant classes.

Throughout the 1930s and '40s, Dehra was a tonga town, the two-wheeled pony-drawn carriage being the principal mode of transport along the narrow roads and lanes that bisected the town. I think there were just two or three motor taxis in Dehra in 1948-49 (as compared to six or seven hundred today), but outside the railway station you would always find a long line of tongas waiting for travellers to descend from arriving trains and proceed homewards, accompanied by the unhurried clip-clop of the ponies. The only unpleasant aspect of the tonga was that if you sat up front near the driver, you would get the pony's fart full in your face; or sometimes the animal would lift its tail and defecate even as you rode along. Still, this was better than the black fumes emitted today by the three-wheelers. These hadn't been invented then but have since put the tongas out of business.

Dehra's narrow roads did not follow any particular pattern but zigzagged all over the place, much in the manner recommended by my Uncle Ken (my mother's younger brother) who once said that the best way to go through life was to zigzag. In that way you saw more of the world and the world saw more of you!

The only really straight roads were Rajpur Road and the Eastern Canal Road; most of the others took off from them and went their own way.

Along these roads were many large compounds with fine old bungalows, flower gardens in front, orchards of lichi, guava, papaya or mango trees at the back. My grandfather had also planted some pomalos (a sort of grapefruit), and these were to survive for many years. I saw a couple of them last year, still giving fruit sixty years after they had been planted. They were my age, those sturdy pomalo trees, and they will in all likelihood outlive me unless someone clears them away.

The big jackfruit tree has gone. It grew just outside the kitchen wall, and later owners removed it to make room for a new cottage. It provided plenty of welcome shade in summer, and also some splendid jackfruits, which were made into curries or pickles.

Dehra was a great place for flower gardens, and the annual flower show (held in March outside the Forest Rangers' College) encouraged competition amongst householders and gardeners. Sweet peas did particularly well and must qualify as my favourite flower, for their heady fragrance if nothing else. Another sweet fragrance is that of the antirrhinum or snapdragon, although it is not so lovely to look at. Petunias were very special, and Californian poppies looked great en masse. Everyone grew roses (or tried to), but somehow Dehra's roses were not in the same class as those grown in Saharanpur, only forty miles away. But then, our geraniums were better! Oddly enough geraniums wouldn't grow in Delhi, 150 miles to the south.

Uncle Ken, who took absolutely no interest in the garden, nevertheless submitted a mass of cut sweet peas to the flower show competition and walked away with a prize and a special commendation. This was typical of Uncle Ken, benefitting from other people's hard work. But he was an affable man and his sisters put up with him. As my mother's three older sisters were all married to fairly affluent husbands (two of them doctors), Uncle Ken would descend on them by turn, apportioning the year between Mhow, Ranchi and Lahore. He never had a job for long, but seemed to manage quite well without one, and he had a way of convincing everyone that he was a handy man to have around the house. In later years, when all his sisters and their families left for England or New Zealand, he had to leave too. As he could not be supported in the same style in England, he had finally to take up a regular job, and the last I heard was that he ended up as a village postman, delivering letters from a bicycle. He was probably quite happy doing this, as he was fond of riding bicycles.

Bicycles were not really my forte and I had two accidents—one a collision with a bullock cart, and the other a tumble as I was trying to avoid Miss Kellner's rickshaw. On this latter occasion I broke my arm, and had to spend most of the winter holidays with my arm in plaster.

I was really a walking person—and was to remain so all my life.

*

It was only a fifteen-minute walk to the Ideal Book Depot, then Dehra's only bookshop of any significance.

I could not afford to buy books but the Ideal Book Depot also had a large lending library, made up of its old or shop-soiled stock. For two or three rupees a week I could borrow as many books as I liked, and in this way I read many of the best-sellers of the time—Betty Smith's *A Tree Grows in Brooklyn,* Priestley's *The Good Companions*, A.J. Cronin's *The Green Years*, William Saroyan's *The Human Comedy*, and practically everything by Wodehouse, in spite of dear Mr Jones's injunctions against his corrupting influence.

It would be true to say that I received a considerable part of my education from the Ideal Book Depot's lending library.

Another escape from the reality of my home life took place in the little Odeon Cinema across the road from the maidan. Whenever I could procure a couple of rupees' pocket money, I would go to the evening show, occupying one of the seats in the cheaper rows. Cinema audiences for English-language films were falling off then, and sometimes there were just a handful of people in the hall. Once, they ran a film for just two people—myself and another regular.

During the intervals, the management always played a couple of records. They had only two or three records, so we had to listen to the same tunes, week after week, month after month. Tiring of this monotony I took some twenty records (mostly Bing Crosby numbers) from the collection at home and presented these to the manager of the Odeon so that he could give us a little more variety during the intervals.

He was so grateful that he gave me a free pass, with the result that for the remainder of my holidays (and the following year too) I was admitted to the cinema on payment of the nominal entertainment tax (four annas) and was able to see as many pictures as I wanted. In this way I became a veritable encyclopedia of information on the movies of the period.

Bliss it was to be able to hide myself away in the Odeon Cinema and be transported to a tropical isle with Dorothy Lamour or shoot up a frontier town with James Cagney or Randolph Scott.

The holiday over, it was back to boarding school once more. But my final year at BCS was a troubled one.

Chapter Nine
The Young Rebel

In 1950, my last year at school, I was the angry young man, in revolt against rules, traditions, conventions, examinations, authority of any kind. Obviously, the effects of the stilboestrol had worn off!

I was sixteen that year, and I felt I was wasting my time in school. Dickens hadn't done much schooling, I reasoned; nor had Jack London or Joseph Cornad or the Bronte sisters or other favourite authors. I had only to write a book and I would be in their glorious company! I'd been given charge of the Anderson Library, and it became my retreat and my private academy. I worked my way though the complete plays of George Bernard Shaw and J.M. Barrie, and devoured the novels of H.G. Wells, J.B. Priestley and the short stories of H.E. Bates, William Saroyan (who had recently burst on the scene) and A.E. Coppard. These last three probably influenced me more than any of the others, because over the years I was to find that the short story or novella best suited my temperament: snatching at life and recording its impressions and sensations rather than trying to digest it whole.

Most of that school year I was in perpetual revolt against authority. This was represented in the person of Mr Fisher, our new headmaster. He was a clever man, with a sharp mind, but he had no children of his own and seemed unable to understand children and their problems. You could confide in Mr Jones and even in one or two of the other teachers, but Fisher seemed to discourage any sort of relationship that would penetrate the invisible barrier he had thrown around himself. His wife was a plum pudding of a woman, who indulged in gross favouritism. The trouble was, this month's favourite would become next month's hate object, and she would go out of her way to make trouble for those who had fallen from grace.

She'd called me a 'doodwalla' (milkman) for letting in a goal during a football match, and I'd retaliated by calling her a 'doodwalli' (milkmaid). For this I was caned, which was fair enough. After all, she was the headmaster's wife.

The food was indifferent that year and some of the boys in my house kept complaining. After all, I was their house captain! And so, the next time Fisher made his rounds of the dining hall, I complained in turn, saying the food was bad and that there wasn't enough of it. It wasn't exactly Oliver Twist asking for more: we were not starved. It was simply William Brown asking for better.[*]

For this, I lost my house captaincy for a time. But I suppose I had a certain amount of charm because I remember my English teacher, Mr Whitmarsh Knight, saying: 'I have a number of reasons for disliking you, Bond, but when I see you I can never remember what they are!'

---

[*] Read the *William* stories by Richmal Crompton.

And then, during the half-yearly exams, I'd submitted a blank answer paper in physics. I was quite hopeless in maths and science but Fisher, who taught the latter, took it as a personal affront. Not only did he give me a zero, he gave me two zeros. I still don't know what two zeros add up to but there must be a rational scientific explanation for them. 0^2 must be more powerful than just 0, I'm sure. Dislike to the power of two equals hate!

Poor Fisher . . . a year later, when I was on my way to England, I heard that both he and his wife had been asked to leave the school—they'd been involved in some scandal or the other. She was the bigger hypocrite of the two; but perhaps the public school system was the biggest hypocrite of all. It set impossible standards for the boys—standards that the staff and administrators could not uphold. For they were frail and faulty humans like the rest of us.

During the next decade my old school went downhill. But I believe it has now recovered some of its old esteem.

*

In December of 1950, I said goodbye to BCS forever, and swore that it was the end of my formal education. Henceforth, it would be conducted on my own in libraries and second-hand bookshops.

Looking back on the eight years of school in Simla, I find there is much to cherish in the memory—the friendships; the old library; the excursions to town. And yet, in India, it was so alien a setting (the 'Eton of the East'), and the life we led so far removed from the reality of the real India and its teeming cities and towns and endless rural horizons, that it did not give me the substance or the inspiration for any of my writing. Not a single story of any significance came out of my schooldays—this is the first time I have written about that period. There was nothing to hide. Worse, from the writer's point of view there was nothin~ to reveal.

School behind me, I was all set to launch myself in the world as a writer. All glory comes from daring to begin!

Did I have any other ambitions? Oh, I would love to have been a tap-dancer like Gene Kelly; or an Arsenal goalkeeper; or a songwriter. But I was realist enough to know that in small-town India in 1951, you could go singin' in the rain but all you got for it was a cold.

There was the maidan, and of course I played a little football there and cricket too, for it was a nice big maidan in those days, without encroachments all over the place. Dehra's population was 40,000. Today it's ten times that! Ah, wilderness, where are you now?

There was one thing I could do in Dehra or anywhere else in the world, and that was write. All I needed was paper and pen or pencil. And that's all I need today. The pencil is my personal computer. All it requires is a good sharpener.

1951 was a watershed in my life; it was to see the genesis of my first novel, and it was to shape my character for the rest of my days.

Of personality I had none; not then, not ever! But I was very much my own person—strong in my likes and dislikes, very stubborn, wanting and getting my own way, my own room, my own privacy; old-fashioned enough to believe in loyalty to friends; *scorning* money for money's sake; ready to discover things about myself and come to terms with a wayward, sensual nature; above all, eager to express myself in the language I'd learnt to love; ambitious enough to want to see my name in print (if not in lights!). To love and be loved; to be free. Free to wander where I pleased; read what I liked; be friends with those who attracted me.

My ambition was tempered by a natural laziness.

Hands in my pockets, I loved to wander about the town: gaze at the film posters; browse at the bookstalls and newsagencies; watch the wrestlers under the old peepal tree; savour the aromas of the bazaar; look at the trains arriving and departing at the station; admire the flowers from garden walls; watch the dhobis washing clothes on the canal banks; study a hoopoe looking for insects on a lawn; wander through the tea gardens; sit beside an irrigation channel and dream; whistle in the spring rain; eat hot pakoras; watch children playing marbles—anything but work!

And yet I did write occasionally—a couple of atmospheric mystery stories in the manner of Peter Cheyney, which duly appeared (to be quickly forgotten) in a little magazine called *My Magazine of India*, published from Madras. I'd first try my stories out on *The Illustrated Weekly of India* or *The Sunday Statesman*. These were the most prestigious publications of the time. There weren't many others, unless you counted *The Onlooker* ('The Onlooker sees most of the game . . .'), a glossy society magazine modelled on the British *Tatler*, which kept you up to date about the more respectable activities of 'high society', chiefly in Bombay; you had to own a racehorse or two in order to be mentioned in its columns.

My rejects (of which there were quite a few) finally found their way into the pages of *My Magazine*, a strange little pocket magazine carrying advertisements for everything, from lucky gemstones to preparations for increasing male potency, all available by mail order. The actual stories were quite harmless, almost respectable, which made me suspect that it was the respectable people who were really interested in activating their sex drive.

My Magazine paid me the princely sum of rupees five per story. Quite rightly they called it an honorarium. I didn't mind. With five rupees I could see three pictures or buy two paperback novels or even a new gramophone record. I received a copy of the magazine every month—gratis, I thought. I'd even sent for a lucky gemstone, which turned out to be a piece of glass. But I took umbrage when I received a money order for two rupees, instead of the usual five, and wrote to the editor, objecting to this unwarranted reduction in my rate of payment. Back came a conciliatory note saying they hadn't reduced my fee, they had merely deducted a year's subscription from one of my payments. I was mollified.

Finally I sold a story to the *Weekly*—it was published later that year—and received a cheque for fifty rupees, which was as much as anyone paid for a story in those days.

*

Before this momentous event, I had acquired a room of my own—a room on the roof of the old Gresham Hotel (now rented out as apartments)—and it came about in this way . . .

I had quarrelled with my mother. I forget what it was about, but I was touchy those days; I think I had been

Father and Mother on their honeymoon, Mussoorie, 1933

Mother and the infant author, in one of the
Kathiawar states, 1935

Father, 1938

Uncle Ken climbs a lamp-post, 1932

Aunt Emily (trying out her lipstick) and Mother with Ellen behind

On the beach, Jamnagar, 1936

Father with three of his pupils,
Jamnagar, 1937

With a friend, Jamnagar, 1937

At a prince's birthday
party, Jamnagar, 1939

Ruskin and Ellen, Jamnagar, 1938

Outside the RAF hutment, New Delhi, 1942

In the foothills near Dehra, 1943

Last picture of Father with a friend and colleague, on a posting to Karachi, 1943

On a visit to Sanawar, 1947

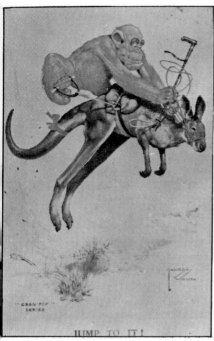

A 'Gran Pop' series postcard sent to Ruskin
by his father

The letter at the back of the postcard

<u>True Copy</u>

<u>Soldier's Name and Description</u>

Name : Herbert William Bond. Born 2-5-1863

Enlisted for the Scottish Rifles on 3rd November 1883, at Bow Street Police Court, London, for 7 years with the colours and 5 years in the reserve, in the County of Middlesex, at the age of 20 years 6 months.

Born in the parish of Islington in the town of London in the County of Middlesex.

Height : 5 ft.6 in. Complexion : Fresh eyes, blue. Hair brown. Religion, Church of England.

———

Marriage : 4-4-1894. Jubbulpore, India. To Gloriana Elizabeth Enever.

———

<u>Children.</u>

9-2-1895. At Hoshangabad Rest Camp. Herbert Henry.

29-7-1896.Shahjehanpur Cantt. Aubrey Alexander.

9-12-1898. Chittagong (Volunteer Hd.Qrs.) Arthur Cleveland.

7-7-1902. Chatham (Fort Pitt). Gloriana Elizabeth.

———

Certified this is a true copy from your (Owen Ruskin Bond's) grandfather's Army Service Book.

Signed: Herbert Henry Bond,
           20/7/65

           40 St.Mark's Road,
           Bush Hill Park,
           Enfield, Mddx.' U.K.

Facsimile of Grandfather's Army service record

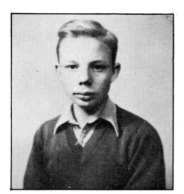

Author, 1948

With the old gramophone and other worldly
goods, New Delhi, 1943

Old and new palaces, Jamnagar, 1938

End of term, BCS, Simla, 1950. A tendency to break the rules

Somi and Chotu, 1951

Haripal on the roof, Dehra, 1957

Ruskin Bond in Jersey, Channel Islands,
1952—the year he began writing
The Room on the Roof

Vu-Phuong, London, 1954

Ruskin Bond at 21 — back in India,
a published author at last!

At a mountain stream, 1959

Author, 1962

Photo: Kamal Kishore

Author, 1963

Author, 1975

Author, 1963

With Rakesh and his son, Siddharth, 1996

With Mukesh, 1980

With Siddharth, Rakesh's son, 1995

Author, 1997

deprived of the use of the radiogram for a few days and had missed my favourite BBC comedy show— *Much-Binding-in-the-Marsh*—to which I had become somewhat addicted; that, and a growing resentment against my stepfather whose business ventures continued to flounder, along with his reputation; and I blurted out, 'Well, I'm not going to live here any longer,' and strode off into the sunset. And that too in late January, when Dehra was reeling under a cold wave, which meant I couldn't sleep in the open, on the maidan. I tried a bench on the platform of the railway station, where other vagrants lay bundled in blankets; but I hadn't brought a blanket, and sharing theirs wasn't a very inviting prospect. So I made my way to the flat of Dr Goyal, whose son, Bhim, a year or two younger than me, had just recently declared himself my friend, philosopher and guide.

He lived up to his declarations, sharing his dinner and small bedroom with me. We spent the night planning my future. I was to make some money by selling anything I had; then I was to find a job.

'But I don't have anything,' I said.

'What about all those books you got as prizes at school,' said Bhim. 'They're as good as new. We'll sell them at half price to Universal—he'll stick his own bookplate over yours, and sell the lot to the St Joseph's library.'

And this was what we did, with Bhim acting as middleman. My new *Complete Shakespeare* (the Hailey Literature Prize), Hesketh Pearson's biography of Dickens (the Anderson Essay Prize) and several other books which had been picked up in the course of an erratic school career, found their way to the Universal Book Shop and eventually the St Joseph's library. The only book I hung on to was George and Weedon Grossmith's *Diary of a Nobody*, which I'd got for acting the part of a tipsy imposter in a one-act play called *Borrowed Plumes*. I had chosen this book myself, at Ram Advani's Bookshop on the Simla Mall. Tommy Handley, a BBC radio comedian, had mentioned that it was his favourite bedtime book, and that was recommendation enough for me. I loved its self-directed British humour, the sort that made *Punch* so popular in its heyday. I have always kept a copy with me.

Of course, Bhim took his commission on the money he got for the books. The rest, about a hundred rupees, lasted for a couple of days. In the company of Bhim and one or two others it melted away. I strolled home and announced to one and all (or to whoever was listening) that I would stay until I found a job; then settled down to a good helping of jackfruit curry and rice.

My mother and stepfather took the whole business very calmly, but it must have worried them, because it was soon after this that I was given my own room—a tiny *barsati*, opening on to the flat roof of the old building. A flight of stone steps ran up to it on the outside of the building. So it had its own entrance and was quite private—except for various birds, squirrels, bats and other small creatures which were also in residence in various corners of that spacious old roof.

A bed, a table and a chair were all that the room contained. It was all I needed—all that any writer needs. Even today, forty-five years later, my room contains the same basic furnishings—only the table is larger, to accommodate more in the way of paper and manuscripts; the bed is slightly more comfortable; and there is a rug on the floor. There is a separate room for my books—a major luxury.

Then, as now, the view from my room, or from its windows, has always been an important factor in my life and in my writing. I don't think I could stay anywhere for long unless there was a window from which to gaze out upon the world.

Of course, I had the entire roof to myself, but the window was important too. It set the scene, so to speak. From my little desk I could look into a bottle-brush tree, and then down the road into the lichi orchard behind old Mrs Wilson's house—over the trees and rooftops, as far as the foothills.

Mrs Wilson's late husband, Charlie, had earned a certain distinction by going to jail for fraud. It was said that he came out of jail a rich man, having bankrupted all his friends and associates. Charlie Wilson's father had been the famous 'Pahari' Wilson, who had made a fortune as the Raja of Tehri's contractor, being the first man to float timber down the Bhagirathi river. This made him the first large-scale exploiter of the forest wealth of this region. He married a village girl and built himself a splendid house at Harsil, eight thousand feet up the river valley. Capitalist villain or pioneering entrepreneur? It depends on how you look at these things. Legend has grown around Wilson but he was no romantic.

The area where the station canteen and other buildings stood had once been a large mango grove owned by the Wilsons, but Charlie had sold or lost most of it, and Mrs Wilson's bungalow was all that remained of a once beautiful estate.

Close by and of more interest to me, was a small bungalow where one of my friends, Ranbir, lived with his sister and mother. His father, a businessman, was away for long periods (another Charlie?) and the rent was often falling due (as, indeed, was ours), but they managed to sustain themselves on his occasional remittances. Ranbir's sister Raj was an attractive, athletic-looking Punjabi girl who enslaved me with one sidelong look from her dark, friendly but fiery eyes. My walks now underwent a sudden change of direction, so that I passed their house at least twice a day. Raj was often in her garden or courtyard, hanging out washing or watering flower beds, and I would stop to exchange a few pleasantries and bathe in the warmth of her frank, appraising gaze. She wouldn't have been called beautiful by those who expect a woman to be completely feminine; she probably had a few male chromosomes in her make-up, giving her the athletic figure that made her so attractive for me. Her face lit up in a smile whenever she saw me, and as no one objected to my visits, they became more frequent and I lingered longer at the hedge that separated her garden from the road. (Yes, we had hedges then, not walls—how times have changed!)

A sewing needle having penetrated her heel and moved some way into her foot, a minor operation was required to remove it. As a result, she had to rest on her bed for a few days. When I enquired about her welfare, I was invited in to see her.

I found Raj reclining, goddess-like, on a *charpai*, one bandaged foot on a pillow, the other elegant bare foot tracing patterns on the wall. She was in cheerful spirits and persuaded me to sit beside her and talk . . . which I did for as long as I could, there being nothing else I could do, with her mother in the next room and Ranbir kicking a football around in the courtyard. I longed to stroke her foot (either foot!) and even gave a hint to this effect, lying that I had taken a course in massage.

Raj said it might be possible later on, maybe when the foot was healed and out of its bandage! The other foot probably needed it too, I observed—there's nothing like a little massage to improve the circulation—but she said she had a headache and would rather sleep, so I went away, expressing the hope that the bandage would soon be removed.

The foot took some time to heal, and my visits grew longer and more solicitous. If patience is necessary to courting a girl, I had all the patience in the world. And Raj was always happy to see me. She allowed me to hold her hand when no one was about, and on one occasion, when her mother was busy in the kitchen, she asked me to put some Oriental balm on her forehead, as she was having one of her headaches. Wonderful stuff, Oriental balm, I have been loyal to it ever since! Using a generous amount of balm, I proceeded to rub it gently into that lovely forehead. Some of it got into her eyes and she cried out and pulled my hands away. I took the opportunity to kiss her eyelids and the palm of her hand.

And that was as far as I got, because Ranbir returned with his cricket bat and ball, demanding that I play with him. Wretched game, cricket, keeping romantic youths out in the sun when they should be indoors, applying balm to the foreheads of feverish young maidens.

But Raj was fond of games too, and when she was better, told me that we should start playing badminton.

Did I play badminton? No, I said truthfully, but I was eager to learn, especially if she was to be my tutor.

I helped her to mark out a badminton court on a bit of wasteland behind the station canteen, and also found some old rackets and a net in Mr Hari's workshop. He had been a badminton player before taking up shikar!

It turned out that Raj had been a badminton champion at school, and as I was a novice at the game, I spent most of the time picking up the shuttlecock and returning it to her. The things we do for love! The scoreline usually went 15-0, 15-0, in her favour. As my game improved slightly, I edged up on her, but she was still beating me 15-2, 15-2! I did not mind. It was lovely to hear her laugh as the shuttlecock whizzed past my ear or caught me in the midriff.

She played barefoot on the dew-drenched early morning grass, and I shall always remember her that way as she darted about the badminton court, lissom, gazelle-like, sparkling in the sunrise. Sometimes I stood still in order to admire her and she would call out, 'What are you staring at? Why don't you play?'

If this were fiction, I would launch into a romantic story. But in small-town Dehra in 1951, you couldn't go anywhere with a girl, unless you wanted to ruin her reputation. You could play badminton with her outside her house, but you couldn't take her to the pictures or to a restaurant without being pursued by callow college students shouting obscenities.

One evening she came up to my room with her brother, and we sat out on the roof, under the stars, and talked of many things. When she left she took my hand in the dark and gave it a squeeze and bit me lightly on the cheek.

Would that she had drawn blood!

We were friends—best of friends—but we could never be lovers.

Chapter Ten

Hold on to Your Dreams

Miss Kellner died that year, and my mother and I attended her funeral, along with the remnants of Dehra's Anglo-Indian/domiciled European community. I was the only young person present.

In a way it was a funeral for everyone, because most of those present knew that it would not be long before they would be laid to rest beside her.

It was a pretty cemetery, with a variety of trees and bushes lining the footpaths, and marigolds and nasturtiums flowering in profusion on the walls and older graves.

It was over a year since I had been to see Miss Kellner, and now I found myself missing her, for she was my last link with the innocence of childhood. An innocent herself (for she could not have had any sexual fulfilment), she had found a playmate of sorts in me when I was a small boy, and although the camaraderie had passed when I entered my teens, I would still go and talk to her about the 'old days' which she recalled so well.

My grandmother had died a couple of years previously (in Ranchi where she had been staying with friends), and the house on Old Survey Road had been sold by her eldest daughter, my Aunt Emily, who had then left the country with her family. Other relatives had also gone away. My mother was the only member of the family left in India.

Most of the boys of my age had already gone away. I was kicking my heels in Dehra, dreaming of becoming a writer, but knowing it couldn't happen overnight. To begin with, you had to have something to write about. Then you had to string words and sentences together in a reasonably interesting and attractive way. A rush of inspiration, and a short essay or sketch could be done. But then you had to type it out, laboriously, on a 1920s Remington, making changes and corrections as you went along, and all this took time. And then you had to find someone to publish it. Tell an editor you were seventeen years old, and he would read no further. So the age had to be concealed. In some of my early stories I took on the role of an old man recalling the loves of his youth, and this seemed to work. 'When I was a young man . . . ' was the opening phrase of many an early tale of romance, and by the time I'd finished writing it I'd be feeling quite ancient! I must have convinced some of my early editors and readers that I was an elderly writer because, when I met one of them a few years later, he exclaimed: 'But I thought you were dead!' And that was a *long* time ago.

I have always enjoyed the company of older people because they have interesting stories and experiences to relate—provided, of course, they do not repeat themselves to the point of boredom. Granny, oddly enough, had never been one for reminiscence, but Miss Kellner had often unburdened herself to me, and so had one or two other elderly people, and this pattern was to continue throughout my life until I became old myself and began running out of older people. And then I turned to children, probably because of their innate wisdom and the thousands of years of civilization in their genes, but with all the freshness of a new life, a new day.

I must have been a sympathetic listener. And in listening I must have absorbed something of the narrator's temperament and attitude, because sometimes I wrote like an older person and sometimes like a child.

I have never got much out of middle-aged people. I'm not sure why. They conceal too much. They are worried about their jobs or their families or their own infidelities and are reluctant to open up lest they compromise themselves in some way. At forty, a man won't tell you about his mistress. At sixty, he'll be happy to tell you all about her. At forty, a woman won't tell you about her secret love, but in her old age she'll be happy to reveal everything. And then it will take on a romantic glow!

After Miss Kellner died there weren't many old people to talk to (not for some time, anyway), because I suddenly acquired a number of young friends.

There was Ranbir and his super sister Raj; there was Bhim, already making little business deals; and there were other families in the mohalla, such as the Lals (who became the Kapoors in *The Room on the Roof*) and the Sikh boys—Haripal, Dipi, Somi and Chotu . . .

Summers in Dehra were hot and sultry and it was hard to stay awake in the afternoons. My mother had lent me a small table fan and I placed it so that its currents blew across my bed where I lay in my underwear till the heat of the day was past.

A turbaned boy of about twelve, smooth-cheeked,

long-legged, wearing a khaki shirt and chappals, stood in the doorway, looking at me as though I were a strange exotic bird, some creature that was about to become extinct. This was Somi, whom I'd already met briefly at his brother, Haripal's house.

He had heard that I was a writer—that I had published a story in the *Weekly*—and was I related to John Ruskin? Because he had to study an essay by Ruskin and couldn't understand a word of it. Would I help? He showed me the essay—an extract from *Sesame and Lilies*, I think—and I couldn't make anything of it either. I protested that I was in no way related to John Ruskin and would never have written anything designed to make life miserable for a struggling schoolboy. And with that we became friends and decided to go on a cycle ride together.

Many were the cycle rides we took along the roads and byways of Dehra—out to the Forest Research Institute and the Military Academy; into the tea gardens along the Hardwar Road; across the dry river bed and through the fields and into the forest. We shared our hopes and dreams; and, sitting by a little canal in the tea gardens, I wrote these lines and tore the page out of my notebook and gave them to Somi. Many years later, when I was going through a difficult period and about to throw in my hand, he copied them out for me and sent them to me from Calcutta, where he was studying for his engineering degree.

> Hold on to your dreams,
> Do not let them die.
> We are lame without them—
> Birds that cannot fly.

91

That was the age to be—seventeen, and with worlds to conquer!

And that was probably why I agreed to go to England to live for some time with my Aunt Emily. The doors of the literary world would be close at hand; I could see my books being published, dozens of them! And there'd be encomiums in the press and I'd be lionized at literary soirées. Perhaps I'd meet some of the great ones—Priestley, Maugham, Mackenzie, Greene—I gathered they were still alive!

Ah, those dreams of youth—so easily snuffed out in most of us, once the going gets rough . . . Would I be able to hang on to them?

*

To give the reader some idea of how I thought and felt and wrote when I was in my seventeenth year, I now give some extracts from the journal I kept in 1951, before leaving for England.

Some of the people described in the journal, such as the Kapoor family, went into my first novel, *The Room on the Roof*. I have omitted these sections and give instead those entries—naive, sentimental but sincerely felt—in which I described my friends (Somi & co. in particular) and some of my neighbours.

Interlude

'The Pure, the Bright, the Beautiful'

The pure, the bright, the beautiful,
That stirred our hearts in youth,
The impulse to a wordless prayer,
The dreams of love and truth;
The longings after something lost,
The spirit's yearning cry,
The striving after better hopes . . .
These things can never die!

Sarah Doudney

From My Journal, 1951

I met Haripal[*] . . . I don't remember how, I think it just

---

[*] Haripal, H.P.S. Ahluwalia, grew up to become one of the first
Indians to climb Everest. Later, during the Indo-Pak war, he
received gunshot wounds which resulted in his being confined to a
wheelchair for the rest of his life.

happened. Probably Ranbir or someone introduced him to me, but I cannot be sure. I know this, that Haripal is one of those people I just had to meet some time or another.

He is, I think, a year younger than me: tall and thin and supple, not powerful but strong. It is his face, the nose, that is so wonderful. I have never met such a big nose—big, not ugly or unshapely, but good-natured . . . artistic. And like it, Haripal is also good-natured.

'What class are you in?' I asked. 'The tenth?'

'Ya. After that I join the Navy.'

'That is horrible . . . I'll never join the forces. There is no freedom, no independence. You take orders from morning to night, and you do all that you do not want to do. At least, what I would not want to do.'

Haripal gave me a tolerant smile. 'And what is your career?'

'It has not begun yet. But I'm going to be a writer.'

'Then you'll have to go to England for that. You've been before?'

'Oh, no. I've been in India all my life.'

'Do you want to go?'

'For the career, yes; otherwise, no. I've got used to this place.'

'I thought you people could never get used to India—the heat, they say, the mosquitoes, the snakes, the beggars, the filth . . . or are you not British? You don't talk like one. In fact, I've never heard your accent before.'

I am proud of my accent. 'It's my own, no one else has it. You don't like it?'

'I can understand it. It is simpler than most. I think you talk bad English just because everyone tries to talk good English.'

Outside, a fruit-seller was crying his wares and

Haripal called him and bought a water melon. He cut open the fruit and, adding salt, we sucked at the soft pink flakes.

'Can you speak Punjabi?' he asked.

'Very badly, *toot-poot* . . .'

He spoke to me in his swift, lilting language, full of expression. The words ran into each other like water into water.

'That's too fast for me,' I said.

'I'll talk slower then . . . You know, I'm very interested in people of other countries. I've got penfriends in Germany, South America and Japan. Only this morning I had a letter from my Japanese penfriend; she is a girl and is just learning English. When you first learn a language it sounds very funny to others.'

He showed me the letter. In the margin were gay sketches, splashes of colour—emerald peacocks, multi-coloured dresses, patchwork sunshades and urns of oriental design. Pretty . . .

The letter went: 'Dear friend, I got your address. I hope you will have me as your letter. I forgive me to be late transmit my letter. To tell the truth. I cannot yet write English.'

It was so simple that it was beautiful.

February 28th

Haripal came to see me, and took me home to lunch. 'I've cooked everything myself, so you have to like it. There is chicken, tandoor ki roti, kulfi . . . you eat Indian food, don't you? Punjabi cooking is the tastiest in the world though, of course, the Bengali will not agree.'

'I eat everything,' I said. 'Does your family know I'm coming?'

'Ya, my mother wants to meet you. I have told her all about you and she says you sound interesting. You are the first English or Anglo friend I have had, you know . . . My sisters are very shy, and they will hide from sight during your first two or three visits; but my brothers are rascals and will not give you any peace.'

His house stood on the outskirts of the town where civilization began to merge with the jungle. It was surrounded by an orchard of peach and plum trees which were covered with pink and white blossoms. A rich red, flowering bougainvillea creeper climbed the walls, and in front of the house were beds of poppies and marigolds. And there were bees and a swallow-tailed butterfly and sunshine.

'It is all Somi's garden,' said Haripal.

'Somi?'

'My brother. He's twelve years old.'

His family was out, so we sat and talked, which is a very easy thing to do with Haripal.

At twelve o'clock a door burst open and a great happiness entered my life.

'This is Somi,' said Haripal.

The boy smiled broadly and said: 'Hallo, Rusky.'

'Hari says you'll do my English homework if I am your friend.'

'Don't be funny, Somi. I never said that.' Haripal's nose assumed a threatening attitude.

'Well, what if you did? I don't want Ruskin to do my homework, I want him to play with me.' He sat on the arm

96

of a chair, rested his chin on his hands, and looked at me steadily for a few moments. 'Don't go.'

'Where?' I asked.

'England. You must stay here. I like you.'

'How can you like me without knowing me?'

'Oh, I know you now . . . Will you like me?'

'Of course.'

'Good, then we'll be best friends.'

He had deep brown, beautiful, dreamy eyes, a broad forehead, a nose like Haripal's but not so big, and muddy hands. The one I shook was warm and firm. His long hair was tied up in a bundle on his head. His features were fair complexioned but hard to notice under the mud that covered them. His feet were bare, his shorts torn.

All this was wonderful but most wonderful of all was the laugh. There was a clear ring to it, and had an echo of its very own.

'Where have you been?' demanded Haripal. 'And why aren't you wearing your turban?'

'I've been digging a hole at the back of the house and the turban is there too.'

'Then go and get it! . . . Wait! Why are you digging a hole?'

'So as to bury the sweeper's dog . . . or do *you* want to bury it? And before I go, I am to tell you that mother and Chotu can't come home for lunch as they are still with the dead dog in the vetrinearly or whatever its name. She says for Ruskin, you and I to start eating . . . And now I'll get my turban.'

He ate little himself but all through the meal kept pressing me to try every dish.

'Ya,' said Haripal, 'you must eat everything or you'll be

97

insulting my cooking.'

'If you did not cook so well I would not get so full so quickly.'

'Wonderful!' cried Somi. 'That is poetry! . . . And now I'm sorry to say I have to go back to the animal hospital to bring the dog for burial. 'Bye!'

He departed as he had arrived; with a bang of the door.

Haripal said: 'Isn't he a chalak, a cunning rascal? Wait till you know him better . . . and you will know him better, be sure. Somi likes you, and once Somi likes a person he will never leave him.'

I went away without meeting the rest of the family for they were busy, I suppose, with the funeral arrangements. But, said Haripal, next time they would all be waiting for me—unless, of course, another dog died.

March 7th

A strong wind blew all day.

It ruffled the trees, whirled dead leaves into the air and, leaving them suspended, took to flirting with the flowers.

I met Chotu, Haripal's other brother, and his mother.

Chotu is three years younger than Somi, still too young to wear a turban, and so his sisters tie his hair up in ribbons. But these he removes as soon as he is out of the gate and, when school is over, he tears down the road on his cycle, his hair streaming behind in the wind. He is very wild, and I like him best with his shirt hanging over his pants and his pants hanging over his knees. He is more demonstrative then Somi but not as deep.

Their mother is a kind, homely woman with refined features, unexceptional except for a familiar slant of the nose. Her friendliness is infectious.

'When Haripal told me about you,' she said, 'he gave me a picture of a red face with horse's teeth. But I like horses and you have got a nice face, more beautiful than Haripal's, anyway . . . You must come to our house whenever you like, it is yours. And, when you are not very busy you can teach Chotu English; he's very lazy and always fails his tests.'

'Oh, that is good!' cried Chotu. 'We'll have fun, Ruskin.'

'And what about me?' Somi said. 'You're not going to teach me?'

'You're too clever to teach.'

'Hm . . . I think you are right. I know, we'll both teach Chotu! Come on, brother, show Ruskin all your dirty books and let him see what an owl you are!'

Chotu jumped for joy and gave me a rough hug.

'Oh, I'm going to learn very hard!'

March 10th

I have a new room, a room on the roof.

It stands at the eastern edge of the building and catches the morning sun the same time as the treetops.

The roof is long and flat, made of concrete, and I can jump out on it if I like or play a game of rounders.

I am writing in it now, on a level with the birds, an eavesdropper on their conversations. I am high up, a little nearer the stars.

One bald myna, the veteran of many a fight, is sitting

on the window sill and watching me with a furtive eye. It hops impatiently from one foot to the other but it has no immediate intention of leaving; it is summing me up, critically, and with experienced eyes. Tonight the tree life will be full of gossip, scandalized at the advent of a human into their domain.

I feel like a monarch. The whole roof is mine, and with it the sun and the stars and the big yellow moon—and yes, that tall tree too, a canopy of scarlet flowers, the blazing flame of the forest.

This room shall be my castle. I shall live in it, write in it, until I must leave it . . . and I think I shall be happy here.

My books, my bed and desk are all that it contains. And, of course, the picture on the wall, a painting of a bowl of flowers, a mixed bunch of wild blossoms, the names of which I do not know. I don't know if there are such flowers and I wonder who painted them. Perhaps it isn't painting; perhaps they just happened.

Mr Mehra, my closest neighbour, lives at the bottom of the stairs. His wife is bedridden. She has a tumour of the brain and is in the grip of a paralysis that has already claimed half her body. It all started three years ago, and last year when she contracted pneumonia, there was little hope that she would live. But she did.

She is dying now . . . But she is living too, she is fighting death. Sometimes, of a night, she throws a fit and screams pathetically, like a wounded animal; her heart beats slowly, heavily, and the family gathers around, waiting for the end.

But in the morning she is still alive, still breathing. The ding-dong battle which can have but one eventual outcome, continues . . .

Mr Mehra has himself become a bundle of frayed nerves. He was rich once, but when his wife fell ill he gave up his job and devoted his time to her bedside. Now he is poor in pocket but not in love.

Day and night he is at the side of his loved one, praying, attending to her wants, never leaving her for more than a few minutes at a time; caressing her, kissing her . . .

And, occasionally, the strain is too much. His will snaps, his brain clouds over. And, suddenly, he will curse his wife and beat her, and cry to God to take them both. Their cries travel far and all the neighbourhood comes to know that Mr Mehra is close to a mental collapse.

There are some who think his wife will live longer than him.

March 15th

It is getting hot. Summer is just around the corner, and at night the mosquitoes come singing in my ears.

Mrs Lal gave me a bottle of citronella oil and told me to rub it on my face and hands to keep the insects away.

I am now keeping my water in a serai, an earthenware flask that keeps the contents deliciously cool. I shall have to hang up a *khus-khus* matting over the door and wet it continually to counter the hot air.

The flies are beginning to put in an appearance, and so are the lizards.

There are two lizards living in my room: they spend the day in a crack in the rafters and emerge at night to feed on the insects that fly round and round the electric light.

For this service I should, I suppose, class them amongst my friends; but I would not like to touch one of them.

Sometimes, losing their hold on the plaster, they fall from the ceiling and land on the floor with a squashy smack; but they don't seem to have any bones to break. Their long red tongues dart out ruthlessly and snatch up a fly, and I begin to feel sorry for the insect. The truth is I am afraid of these dirty brown, slithery reptiles.

And it is all Mrs Lal's doing.

She told me of an entire family that died because a lizard had fallen into the cooking pot and been cooked with the food. A doctor died when one fell on his knee and bit him! And Mrs Lal says she very nearly swallowed one herself when it slipped into her glass of water.

So Mrs Lal says . . . and even if it is all fabrication, I am very timid.

It is an effort to get out of bed in the morning. I just want to lie down all day and drink cold water. In the afternoon I get under a tap and bathe; and immediately after I am overcome by a spell of drowsiness and lie down on the grass under the mango tree and sleep till six.

It was at six that Chotu came for a lesson in English. Running up the stone steps and on to the roof, he shouted, 'Ruskin, where are you living, in the trees? I could not find you until the people downstairs told me where . . . See, I have come as promised!'

'How are Haripal and Somi?'

'Good, good. Haripal has gone to school to play hockey. And Somi is coming to see you this evening after you have made me clever. Let us start by reading the story of Rumplestiltskin; it's my favourite.'

He sat down at my desk and I stretched myself out on my bed.

Chotu's reading was slow and laborious, and he paused at every second word, unable to make it out; but there was expression in his voice and, better still, enthusiasm. He rejoiced with the characters of the story and wept when they wept.

' "The—Prince—saw—the—Princess—at—the—mouth—of—the—cave!" . . . Ruskin, how does a cave have a mouth?'

'Isn't your mouth a sort of opening into your face? So why not call the opening of a cave a mouth?'

'All right . . . "She-had-piles . . ." ' He stopped, looked at me quizzically and grinned. 'Ruskin, what are piles?'

'Give me the book,' I said. 'Piles, indeed! I thought as much . . . "She had piles of jewels lying all around her . . . " When there is no full stop, Chotu, then do not stop. Now read on.'

But down below I heard a cycle drop to the ground, and in a minute Somi filled the room.

'You've finished?' he asked.

'We've just started,' said Chotu, 'but it's enough for today. Ruskin taught me many new things.'

We·went out to explore the roof, and climbed the topmost terrace. Somi stood up on a chimney and surveyed my domain. 'You should make a garden up here.'

I thought it was a wonderful idea. 'Will you help me if I make one?'

'Of course. I know where to get good seeds.'

'Me, too!' cried Chotu, very excited. 'I'll bring the mud!'

We began making plans, marking out the roof for the positioning of flower beds, deciding on the sunny spots. Suddenly, Somi went right off the point and remarked, 'Are you rich, Ruskin?'

'That's a funny question,' I said. 'No, I'm not rich.'

'Most white people in India are. My brother says this is where they got rich . . . Would you like to be rich?'

'I suppose so, a little. And you?'

'A little . . . Do you like money, Ruskin?'

'Yes. But I don't love it.'

'Neither. It is useful but it is not good. That is what the holy man told me, the rishi . . . '

'What else did he tell you?'

'He said, what is the use of collecting money, for when we die we cannot take it with us; and if we have it while we live, then it gives trouble. He said it is unfriendly because everyone wants to be its friend.'

We were silent a little while and I thought when one is rich the thrill of giving is not as great as when one is poor; for generosity is expected of a rich man, though it is rare when it comes. But when a poor man gives, it is something to be remembered. I think the golden rule is to save a little, spend a little, give a little, but to have it as a constant companion is dangerous.

The silence was broken by Somi. He said, 'Rich people love money—we, we love life.'

March 24th

Somi and I began work on the roof garden, and in honour of the occasion he played truant from school.

'Won't you get into trouble?' I asked.

'No, I was sent out of class. I did not wear my school uniform this morning, so they've sent me home to put it on.'

'And aren't you going to do that?'

'No, I'll say I tore the pants on the cycle.'

We made an inspection of the waste ground in the compound and, finding a spot where the earth was dark and soft, began to dig—Somi with a toy spade and I with a poker. We had nothing else, no shovel, pickaxe, fork or spade.

But our problem was soon solved. Chotu suddenly appeared in our midst and in his arms was a dog.

It was a terrier of sorts, with a touch of daschund and a retriever's tail. Its ears were mangy, its hair scruffy. But it had a face full of expression, eyes that were full of mischief.

'See, he will dig for you,' said Chotu, going down on all fours himself and scraping at the hole we had made. 'His name is Prickly Heat . . . rats, rats!'

The mongrel yelped joyfully and dashed at the hole, pawing, scraping, scooping up mounds of mud. Chotu manned a bucket, Somi a watering can, and I an old flowerpot, and together we filled them with earth.

We climbed the steps to the roof in relays, Prickly Heat running around us and barking furiously, his tail revolving in a complete circle.

'Rats, rats!' cried Chotu, and the dog would return to the hole and dig furiously.

It was a tiring business carrying bricks and rocks up the steps but Kishen came to our aid and our ranks increased.

Ranbir passed by, sceptical, aloof. 'You are mad' was all he said. 'Come and play cricket.'

We had laid out two beds before the sun set. Our hands were muddy, scratched and blistered.

'That is all for today,' announced Somi, 'but I'll plant the first seeds before I go.' He sprinkled a few over one of the beds.

'What were they?' I asked.

'Pumpkins.'

I was indignant. 'But I don't want vegetables, I want flowers.'

'You can have flowers . . . What's wrong with vegetables? We can eat them.'

'Yes, but how will it look, marigolds and pumpkins all mixed up!'

'Very nice,' said Chotu. 'Very nice.'

The trees became very noisy as Somi and Chotu were about to go. 'The birds are talking about us,' said Somi. 'They also think we are mad.'

We have made it a custom that I carry Somi and Chotu down the steps piggyback whenever it is time for them to go home. Somi leapt on my shoulders and wound his arms so tight around my neck that I could scarcely breathe. 'Fast down the steps,' he said. 'Come on, my donkey, my *tuttoo*, gallop hard or I'll whip you! Fast down the steps and do not fall . . . Oh Ruskin, you're a nice chap . . . you are my favourite friend.'

From the roof I saw them peddling home, down the road, between the trees; once they turned and waved and called goodnight, and then they went round the corner.

Chotu's lesson has been forgotten. The room is in a mess.

Mud and bricks and tufts of grass are scattered about the floor, and the watering can has overturned in the centre of the room and I wade across to my bed.

All this I do not mind for Somi and Chotu are the two

106

most wonderful boys in the world; but I wish they had not left Prickly Heat under my bedsheets.

March 26th

Haripal introduced me to his cousin, Dipi, who is a year younger than him, quiet and a little shy. But there was friendship in his eyes as he shook me by the hand.

'I am happy to be your friend,' he said.

His features are fine, noble in their clarity. Like Haripal, he is long-limbed and supple. His legs, in contrast to the rest of his body, have been burnt dark by the sun, for he hates trousers and socks. The Haripal family never wears anything longer than short pants, spurns socks and prefers sandals and slippers to shoes.

They took me home to try some of their experimental ice cream. It was in pinks and whites, greens and oranges, but it all tasted the same to me; very nice. They added almond and pistachio nuts, giving it a novel flavour.

'Good?' said Haripal.

I said, 'Good!'

'That's good,' said Dipi. 'One day we'll cook a meal in your room and have a picnic on the roof.'

Outside a storm broke loose. The air had been still and sultry, the sky tense, overcast; and after the first deep rumble of thunder the hailstones clattered down upon the corrugated tin roof.

The heavens were electrified with sudden shafts of light. The blanket of black cloud groaned and wept heavily. The flowers bent beneath the weight of the hail and broke and fell. Water rushed down the drainpipes and joined the stream that had formed in the garden, and the puddles deepened every minute.

'The crops will be spoilt,' said Haripal, 'and the farmers will say the gods are angry. They certainly sound angry.'

Dipi said, 'This means that summer is really here. Now it won't rain again till the monsoon, so be thankful for this.'

The electricity had failed, and so we sat in the darkened room and looked out on the garden. The hailstones, as big as marbles, continued to rattle overhead, drowning our conversation.

Soon we were silent, and nature did all the talking.

May 1st

It is hard to capture the mood of summer's heat on a day like this, for the sky is sombre, there is a light drizzle of rain and a cool breeze, scented with honeysuckle and jasmine and something else, blows through the open door.

The calendar says it is May, but I think it is lying. Yet it was only yesterday that the blazing sun kept me inside, with a wet towel wrapped round my head; but today it is all so different . . . Still, it *is* summer and tomorrow I shall really know it.

Down below, the rose bushes are taking time off, and there are only a few withered, dirty-looking blooms left over from last month. I, too, feel dirty and sticky, and a little drugged.

But up here in my own garden there are small green shoots, and I am very thrilled for I never expected to see anything at all.

And there is another consolation for this season—the fruit! The lichi trees are covered with soft, round, juicy, brown-skinned fruit; and in another week the mangoes will be ripe enough to eat.

There is no fruit so passionate as a mango; its rich, golden caress oozes with sensuality.

The grass has not quite made up its mind whether it should stay yellow or turn green, and I think it will have to remain this dirty colour until the monsoon arrives and settles the matter.

The banyan tree, which is the one on a level with my room, has now added a woodpecker to its tenants, and I hear the bird tapping away every morning. The squirrels arch their striped back, sniff the air, and scamper into some mysterious forest of leaves. I could live in that tree just as well as I do here; I could, in fact, build a house *in* that tree.

This is the season during which nature has its full share of life while we poor people must fortify ourselves against the sun and insect world.

A pink bougainvillea creeper, not as striking in colour as Somi's but not bad either, has crawled up the wall of the building and sent a shoot in through my window. Now I must not shut the window.

Yes, summer has its compensations.

Shade, for instance, and an iced drink of fruit juice; the opportunity of being lazy, of sleeping all afternoon and waking up fresh; of knowing how welcome is a cool breeze; of watching the fly-paper doing its business; and of wearing as few and whatever clothes I like, and feeling the exquisite shock from a bucket of cold water.

And the fruit, the fruit!

May 5th

Mrs Mehra, the sick lady, was laid out on her string bed under the banyan tree. Her husband was sitting beside her when I passed by and she called me by my name. 'Good morning, Ruskin!' It was a querulous greeting.

Mr Mehra was delighted. 'She is better. See, she wants to talk to you, she knows who you are. Please talk to her, Ruskinji.'

'Good morning, Mrs Mehra,' I said, approaching the bed. 'How are you today? Feeling better?'

'Yes, thank you . . .' She was silent a while and a tear trickled down her cheek; then she turned her head and spoke to her husband in Punjabi.

'She does not speak English very well,' explained Mr Mehra. 'But she wants to know why you and other boys were taking bricks and mud upstairs.'

'Oh, we were making a garden.'

'How wonderful!' exclaimed Mr Mehra and told his wife of it. She smiled, and her big sad eyes glistened in excitement.

Slowly, she said, 'Give me flowers.'

To Mr Mehra I said: 'Tell her that I will give her flowers as soon as they grow.'

He was enjoying the game, supremely happy because his wife was a little better, though he must have known that it was not to last. 'She says when she is better she will cook you good things to eat.'

'Then I hope it will be soon.'

'She says you remind her of her son.'

'I am very happy to give her such thoughts. Where is her son now?'

'He died.'

Mrs Mehra was crying softly, pathetically, and her husband said, 'She cries because just now she is happy. God will make her well soon. Pray for her, Mister Ruskin, pray for her; she has fought so hard for life that death would not be fair, though it would be a merciful thing.'

It would be merciful. It would end all suffering. But no, it would not be fair.

May 19th

I enter my seventeeth year and for the first time in my life celebrate with a party.

Kishen and I did everything. We made ice cream from blancmange powder, and bought lemonade, Indian sweets and English confectionery, and collected plates from all our neighbours. Up on the roof we spread out my bedsheets and laid out the tea.

No grown-ups were invited. Ranbir was detained in school, so there came Haripal, Somi, Dipi, Chotu, Kishen and, of course, the crows.

The birds begin before us and remove the sandwiches while I am receiving my friends at the door.

Chotu says, 'I've brought Prickly Heat to the party. Do you want him as a birthday present, Ruskin?'

I say, 'No, I don't want any presents. Come and eat.'

'Hey!' cried Chotu. 'The birds are finishing our party; shoo, Prickly, shoo!'

The dog went for them and scattered birds, plates and bottles. Kishen was annoyed. 'Damn, the dog has gone and stood on the cakes. It might as well finish them now.'

We sat on the ground which was burning hot, and ate ice cream which was getting hot and had long ago left the ice age. Haripal looked at it suspiciously and said, 'What is this?'

The ice cream stared back at Haripal, and Kishen and I looked at each other. 'It's pudding,' answered Kishen with a shrug of the shoulders.

'Ice cream pudding,' I added. 'Made for the first time in the history of cooking by myself. That's something you can't make, Haripal.'

He could not eat it, either.

Kishen steered the conversation away from ice cream. 'I say, Somi, don't throw lemonade about, it will go through someone's window!'

That was what it did. Mr Mehra's voice came up from below. 'Mister Ruskin, what's happening! Please don't plant any seeds near my skylight. When you water them my wife gets wet!'

I called back, 'I'm very sorry, Mr Mehra. The watering can fell over. There are no flowers near the windows.'

'That's all right, Mister Ruskin,' he shouts. 'Carry on with the gardening, I want to see the flowers soon.'

Somi was peering down a chimney, holding a bottle in his hand.

'I hope you are not throwing lemonade down there,' I said anxiously.

He looked very amused. 'Don't be funny, Ruskin. Who'd think of pouring lemonade down a chimney. I'm only dropping the bottles down.'

May 25th

I slept till late in the morning and then wallowed in bed for an hour after I had opened my eyes.

Last night I stayed up till midnight, writing . . . I wrote two poems, one long and one short, and began a story.

It is a bad story.

I don't know if I am a good writer, there is no one to tell me. I doubt even a critic will ever find time for saying I am good or bad. I get pleasure and satisfaction from writing but that does not mean that what I write is good and interesting. My style is jerky, too impatient; because I am impatient, rushing from one emotion to another, losing sequence.

But it does not matter, I am happy . . .

I was visited by a laugh and it brought Somi with it.

There is something of the elf about Somi, so different is he from ordinary human beings. He is what I sometimes dream about, and he is a dream come true. I knew him long before we met . . .

'You are still my favourite friend,' he told me while we ate spiced cucumbers on the roof.

'I am proud of it,' I said.

'You should be.' He pushed a fallen branch in through an open skylight. 'I love you, Ruskin. I love you as much as I love Chotu and Prickly Heat. I think maybe I love you even a little more than that.'

June 10th

I felt sticky and restless all afternoon and removed my

shirt and vest, shoes and socks. After sitting at my desk an hour without completing a sentence, I flung myself on the bed and fell asleep.

It was Somi who woke me, trying to force the neck of a lemonade bottle between my lips.

'Drink,' he said. 'You are looking tired. At first I thought you had fainted.'

'I was only sleeping.'

'Yes, I watched you for five minutes. You make noises like my grandfather but not as loud. Every time my grandfather breathes, his moustache flutters. The flies do not come near him . . . but come on, let's go out!'

'No, Somi, I'm too lazy to get dressed now. Sit and talk.'

I am becoming too lazy for anything.

Perhaps I am rotting here, perhaps the West will do me good. I have achieved nothing. I have achieved nothing but happiness.

But I must not give way to ambition, else I shall lose that happiness. One day there will come a time of rush and work and worry, and then I shall long for this peace, this idleness, this present.

I must not forget how to be lazy. Dear Reader, nearly fifty years on I'm still very lazy.

June 14th

The earth was blessed with rain.

It came down in sheets, and I was so thrilled that I stripped and ran out on the roof.

There is nothing so exhilarating as a rain bath. The water streamed down my body, swept against it by a cool, tingling breeze that soon sprang into a strong wind. I was driven inside.

The water entered my room from under the doors and through the skylight, and there was no preventing it from flooding the floor. I took to bed as I would to a desert island in a stormy sea.

Outside, the trees bent their backs and shook their heads like wet dogs. And across the compound I saw a shirt, Kishen's I think, being swept off a clothesline and carried over the wall.

July 4th

Dust.

It blew up in great clouds, swirling down the roads, clinging to everything it touched. Burning, choking dust.

Then rain . . .

Out of the dust came big, black rumbling clouds. A lonely drop first, on the window pane, then a patter on the glass, a shower . . . Then the downpour, drumming on the roof.

Chotu ran up my steps with Prickly Heat behind. 'Barsaat!' he cried. 'It is the monsoon, Ruskin, the rainy season has begun! No lessons today!'

From the stronghold of the bed we watched the play of water. Prickly Heat left the flooded floor and shook his coat out on my blankets, then rubbed his nose on the pillow.

The trees bent low like old women, the flowers lay flat and crushed. Everywhere doors kept banging. A cyclist, caught unawares by the deluge, rode home furiously, swishing through the wide, curving sweep of wind and water.

The drainpipe coughed and choked, and the swelling gutters flooded out the roads. The lean trees swayed, swayed, bent with the burden of wind and water.

The rains at last.

And when it stops, a chorus of frogs, croaking happily in the slush. The birds take up their conversation at the point where the elements interrupted, and Prickly Heat slips out of the room.

A gleam of sun?

Oh, no. More thunder.

Down again, the wind and water, all-embracing rain.

Mr Mehra knocked gently on my door. 'Excuse me, Mister Ruskin, but I have a great favour to ask of you. You do not mind?'

'Of course not, Mr Mehra.'

'My wife . . . well, she is very hurt because you passed by today and did not say good morning . . . Ah, ah, Mister Ruskin, I know, I know; you did not mean it, you are too kind to ignore my wife. But she does not understand that sometimes your mind is busy with other things and that you do not notice your surroundings. Often I have seen you dreaming in the daytime. . . . This I tried to explain to her, but she—she is funny, she thinks you are angry with her. Just come down and say good morning, Mister Ruskin, then she will be happy.'

Mrs Mehra was resting in her usual place under the banyan tree. Her cheeks were damp.

I approached unhurriedly, casually, eager that she should not feel I had come through pitying politeness.

'Good morning, Mrs Mehra,' I said breezily as I passed

by on some imaginary business.

'Good morning, Ruskin,' she said and her wet face broke into a smile.

I have never had many friends. These few here are the sum total: Haripal's family, Kishen's family, Ranbir and my neighbours.

I think I like being lonely; it makes friends more welcome. Sometimes I talk to myself . . . intelligently, I'm sure! I hate a crowd of acquaintances; I hate the casual, jocular sort of friend and the noisy backslapper. I call friends those for whom I have an affection, for whom no sacrifice is too great; and because I have not a multitude of them, I value the few. They are the necessities of my life.

July 10th

Is life worth living? That, said someone anonymous, depends on the liver.

Mine has made the last week miserable.

'You are looking very thin,' commented Mrs Lal.

'Eat more vegetables,' advised Ranbir's mother. 'Drink dahi. It will take your pimples away.'

'Don't eat fat.'

'Drink lots of water.'

'Carrots.'

'Plenty of fruit.'

'Mangoes.'

'Not at all. Oranges.'

'See a doctor.'

'No, don't see a doctor . . . '

117

And Ranbir says alarmingly, 'What have you been doing with yourself?'

There is only one cure for a sluggish liver. I dug Haripal out of his house, and together we went to the pictures. That settled me and my liver. It was Laurel and Hardy.

July 20th

Chotu, wearing a turban for the first time in his life as a sign of advancing years (he is eight, I think), announced that from today there would be all play and no work. My tuition has been unsuccessful, for he has failed his examinations again.

September 10th

In the early hours of the morning I heard the sound of voices and running feet.

'Call the doctor!'

'It's too late!'

'God help us . . .'

And above the excited clamour of voices, Mr Mehra's rose shrilly. 'She is dying . . . dying . . . my wife, God save her. But where is the doctor? Call him, call him!'

I leapt out of bed and came out on the balcony. Down below a group of people pressed round Mr Mehra's door, all talking confusedly.

There was a hush when the doctor's car drove up, and the people made way for him.

'Please go to your homes,' he requested. 'It will not help

if you crowd round the door, the patient must breathe.' It was the same doctor who had attended Kishen's bicycle accident; his air of authority caused the spectators to retreat but did not dispel them. In silence, they watched from a discreet distance.

I could hear the heavy breathing of Mrs Mehra. I could hear her heart thumping, slowly, painfully, and every now and then she would give a deep, long drawn-out sigh.

The doctor was busy for at least fifteen minutes, and all the while the group of people remained outside in a cluster, waiting, whispering . . .

When the doctor came out, Mr Mehra fell at his feet. 'Is she better? For God's sake, is she better?'

'She is better for the present. But tell these people to go home, even if they *are* relations.'

September 12th

Somi wanted to eat spiced cucumber and I coconut, and as we both wanted our own way we had words. At first we quarrelled in play, but this gave rise to irritation.

'Go and eat your blinking coconut,' said Somi. 'You can eat it all by yourself.'

'And you,' I replied, 'can eat your damned cucumber alone!'

Somi said, 'Goodbye, I'm not coming to see you again,' and left the room.

I laughed. Then I became alarmed.

I rushed out on the balcony and shouted, 'Hey, Somi, come back!' But he had gone.

Depression . . . I threw myself on the bed and stared at

the ceiling. A lizard chased another along the rafters.

I shifted my gaze to the open door and saw two crows knocking each other's feathers out.

'What's wrong today?' I wondered. 'Everywhere there is temper.' I felt slightly disillusioned; perhaps I am too possessive with my friends, wanting my own way too much, wanting them too much.

Life seemed an empty dream, full of nothing but self-pity and foolishness.

'Oh Somi,' I whispered to myself, 'I spoke to you in fever, not anger, but the words bled our friendship; and now remorse is choking me. Oh hell, I'm unhappy!'

The crows ceased their discordant quarrel, and in the ensuing stillness I heard the lizards scuttling about above. The white ceiling shimmered in the sunlight. Everything began to shimmer.

I dreamt I was learning to swim. I could swim, I could keep myself afloat, but I was unable to move forward; only backward. Somi was in the water too, ahead of me, out of reach, with a balloon tied around his neck. I called to him to wait till I caught up but the balloon faded and became a coconut.

And I opened my eyes and there was a coconut before them, with Somi behind it, shouting to me to wake up. 'Eat your coconut,' he said and ruffled my hair. 'Your hair is like the hay that horses eat.'

I said, 'Oh Somi, you should have bought a cucumber instead. I was only joking but you got angry.'

He showed me a cucumber. 'I, too, was only joking, but *you* got angry. And don't worry, I've bought a cucumber for myself. You eat your blinking coconut and I'll eat my blooming cucumber!'

120

September 14th

I was quite right, autumn *is* here.

My mind is troubled, yet I feel tranquil.

The rain has swept over the hot dry land, cleansing the sky and earth of dust and dirt; it has been and gone like a soft hand running over smooth silk. I saw it flirt in the arms of trembling trees, kissing the leaves, bathing the earth . . . And now the warm sun bathes us in gold.

The dew on the grass smells sweet, and the rose bushes glisten in the mellow sunlight. Dreamily, I listen to the exhilaration of birds, which fills the air with autumnal song.

The summer has gone, my last Indian summer. And this is the last autumn.

A month, only a month, and I shall leave with the autumn, this saddest, most beautiful season. I try not to think ahead, I try to drown the future in my ever present past, but it looms before me all the time, approaching nearer. I wish time could stand still, now, this very minute, and that life could carry on this way. But my accursed ambition will not have it.

In a rushing, materialistic world of doers I shall most likely be a failure, and I'll be sorry for ever having given up this life. I can write here—anywhere—but it is the desire for recognition and applause that lures me away. I tell myself that fame is not greatness, and that if I remain as I am long enough I shall soon grow accustomed to obscurity. At least I shall retain my individuality, and in art that is most important.

In the West I shall start following this trend and that, fashions and styles and topicality. I shall probably emerge a hack, one of thousands.

I can still write if I remain here, even though few will read my work; and there, who knows, nobody might read me.

October 2nd

A little lonely. And, suddenly panicking at the thought of leaving in a few days, I hurried to Haripal's house.

They were all at home. Somi was digging in the garden and Chotu sat in the branches of a guava tree, collecting guavas.

'Come and eat with me,' he invited. His hair was wild and his feet muddy and scratched. I have yet to see a healthier specimen of youth than Chotu when he is untidy and rough.

'I'm too heavy for those branches,' I replied.

'All right, I'll break the guavas for you.' He threw the fruit down to Somi and me; it was green but sweet.

'We'll get sick if we eat too much,' I warned him.

'This is my tenth today,' bragged Chotu. 'Food cannot make me sick.'

With Haripal, we strolled down to Dul's* house and found him in bed.

'What's this, what's this!' exclaimed Haripal. 'He's sleeping in the day.'

'I've got fever,' groaned Dul.

'Then, tell us, why have you been eating chaat? Come on, get up, you fat, lazy lump of plasticine!' He took Dul

---

* Dul (Daljit) joined the Indian Air Force after finishing school. He lost his life during a training flight.

by the feet and dragged him from the bed; then we pulled him down the road in his pyjamas.

There was much merrymaking. Haripal cooked us a meal and afterwards, Somi, Chotu and I sat on the couch while Chotu read the story of Rumplestiltskin, which is his favourite, the only one in his reader which he has mastered. He never tires of it.

Somi was unusually silent and serious.

'What's wrong?' I asked him. 'Why are you so quiet?'

'I am thinking . . .'

'Of what?'

'Of you. If you go away, Ruskin, I will be sad.'

'I'll come back.'

'You won't. You will forget us.'

'That's impossible . . . I don't want to go but I must. I'll write to you every week. I'll send you anything you want. You and Haripal and Chotu, for you I'll do anything; you are my brothers.'

'You will do everything except come back.'

There is nothing awkward about Somi's sentiment, every gesture of his is natural and spontaneous. I am the clumsy one.

He said little but he took my hand, and his eyes and his hands spoke all. They would not leave me, not even when I had passed from sight.

His warm, dirty, comfortable hands . . . Haripal's expressive nose, Chotu's wild exuberance, Dipi's fond fussing, Dul's amiable rotundity . . . these I do not want to lose.

But these I must lose.

October 3rd

When I am with Dul I am contented, for with him there is never any need for speed or hurry. We amble. We idle.

Unlike Haripal, who is forever on the move, and Dipi, who never stops fidgeting, Dul has a zest for inactivity. I am lazy but not idle; I work hard in a leisurely manner. But Dul is perfect. He can sit and talk and never bother to get up at all.

October 11th

It is pneumonia, Haripal tells me . . . Somi is in bed with high fever and a pain in the chest. He talks with difficulty, for the cough takes hold of him when he tries to speak. But he managed to say, 'Get me a water pistol, Ruskin . . . I will be all right before you go.' He squeezed my hand and looked into me and was still looking into me when he closed his eyes and slept.

Why must this happen as I am about to leave? Why now, now, when I cannot stay here and help him? Three days remain . . . and I cannot hope for a recovery in such a short time. I'll leave in an agony of uncertainty; restless, unhappy . . . Perhaps I will not leave at all.

I told Haripal this; I told him I would not go. He said: 'But you must, Ruskin, this will be your only chance. Don't worry about Somi. He'll get better, I know it. He is too fond of life to let it go. It won't help by your staying. Somi will be all right, I tell you.'

'Oh, I don't know what to do.'

'You must write to him. That will make him happy. It

will not be good if you let him think you have forgotten
us!'

'I will write, Hoppa,' I said. 'Every week of my life . . .
And if I don't, then you'll know I'm dead. How can I forget
when I do not want to . . .'

I do not want to. I cannot.

And tomorrow the partings begin. Dipi goes camping
with the school cadet corps, and he will say goodbye in the
morning.

I think it is easier this way, easier on the heart; rather
this than all together, everyone saying goodbye at the
same time.

October 12th

I could not sleep. I rose early, dressed and paced the roof.
The morning was silent, breathing still air, the roof wet
with dew. The trees still slept.

I saw Dipi climb the stairs and went to meet him.

'I must report at school in half an hour,' he said. 'We'll
take a walk.'

The white lines of the neglected badminton court still
showed on the grass. I noticed this as we passed out of the
gate and made for the maidan.

The town showed its first signs of life: cows and dogs
amongst the dustbins.

October 13th

Somi is a little, little better. He looked frail, his face pale
and tired; but he could talk.

'If I were well I would come with you,' he said.

'It is better here, Somi. And you are coming with me, you are coming in my heart. You don't think I'll forget you, do you?'

'We won't let you forget. When you come back we'll never let you go again.'

His mother took me aside and said, 'Do you need anything, my child?'

'Yes,' I answered. 'Lots of love.'

'You have that. You belong to our family. That is why I ask you if you need anything.'

'I need nothing, Mataji.'

But I did. I needed courage. I saw, for the first time, the tribulation lying ahead, the toil, the task, the sweat and blood; the hate, the frustration, the hopelessness, misunderstanding, malice . . . I felt incapable of facing the future. I felt small, weak . . . and all I wanted to do was lie down in the haven of Haripal's house and never, never venture out.

I did not want to face the world.

Somi's mother took my face in her hands and I cried. 'Be brave,' she whispered. 'Somi says you are very brave.'

But Somi is braver than me . . .

The Fourteenth and Last Day of October

I made my last visit to the house of Haripal.

We gathered in the front room, his family, Dul and Kishen. Somi was better but wrapped in blankets in an armchair.

'See,' he said, 'I'm all right now. I can say goodbye to you properly.'

Haripal said, 'You'll have to say it here, though. You're not strong enough to come to the station tonight.'

Somi said nothing. He was in high spirits and winked at me.

We were cheerful. I did not think but cast off my moods and doubts, and considered instead how lucky I was to have ever had such friends. For once I realized how young I was, how old I had tried to be and thought I was, and for once I appreciated my youth.

I have never seen Dul so lively before. He lathered his hands with soap and wiped them on my face; so we sat on him and smeared polish on his.

Haripal said, 'You and I are brothers, Ruskin. Take whatever you want; it is yours to remember us by.'

'You're talking like a rich maharaja,' I said. 'But I have already taken what I want. I have had it a long time, ever since we met. I am taking with me the remembrance of you—and so I take everything.'

I felt slightly feverish when I returned to my room to pack my worldly possessions, my books and clothes. Mostly books, for I have always been indifferent to what I wear. Resting on the bare bed I looked up at the lizards. Callous creatures, unconcerned with my departure . . . to them one human is just the same as any other.

And the bald myna, hopping in and out of my flower beds, will continue to hop and fight and lose more feathers; and will gossip about the next inhabitant of this room as enthusiastically as she gossiped about me. And the crows and the squirrels, will they miss me? Hardly. It is quite true, one human is no different to any other, though we may not think so.

And the garden . . . It is finished now, the flowers are

withering, mourning with dry, drooping heads. I am proud of them. They and I shall leave the roof together. They end their life and I end one phase of mine. They turn to seed and I begin to sprout.

I paid my last respects to Mrs Lal, Ranbir and his sister. They would not believe I was leaving.

'You're bluffing,' said Mrs Lal. 'You never told us before.'

'I'm going to the station now,' I said.

Raj looked up from the mirror she held in her hand. She was combing her hair and it hung down to its full length, filling the air with perfume, reminding me of the actress Nimmi.

'Ruskin is up to his old tricks again,' she said.

Ranbir said, 'You will never leave this place. You have got stuck in that room of yours, with your garden and your typewriter.'

Somewhere, a radio was turned on. Ranbir said, 'My request will be played today,' and slipped into his house.

There was nothing I could do but go. 'Think what you like, but I tell you this is the last you see of me.'

Raj caught me by the ears as I tried to kiss her, and I wish, oh I wish, she had never let them go.

Raj laughed. 'Well, goodbye, *Mister* Ruskin; good luck—till tomorrow.'

But tomorrow is three hundred miles away.

They came to the station; my friends, my brothers. We stood together outside my compartment while around us the coolies pushed and struggled, the vendors cried their wares and the flies outnumbered all. Two dogs moved around in a circle, sniffing at each other's tail; another raised its hind leg and watered a lamp-post. Everywhere noise and lights and smells; and smoke and dust; and filth and beauty. Oh India, my India, for all your dust there is a blossom.

I stroked Haripal's nose. 'Everything is lovely tonight, Hoppa. Your nose, it is the most beautiful nose in the world. I shall miss it.'

The nose registered Haripal's disapproval, for he is not sentimental. 'I'm glad you are going. When I see you again, you'll be a big, important man.'

Chotu clung to me excitedly. 'Send me stamps. Send me pictures. And ribbons for Prickly Heat!'

Somewhere a whistle blew and a gong sounded. The noise and rush increased.

Haripal and Kishen shook me by the hand and Dul flung his arms around my neck and embraced me.

'I look a fool,' he said. 'But so what? We are both fools.'

I stepped on to the moving train. I stood at the door. The little group of four stood together, waving desperately; receding, falling from my reach . . . Haripal's loping gait, Chotu's brawling affection, Dul's wink . . . drifting away with the wave of a hand.

Four . . .

Five!

Tearing along the platform, helter-skelter, shouting at the top of his voice, came Somi.

He drew level with the carriage before the engine gathered speed.

'Goodbye, Somi!' I shouted.

'Goodbye, Ruskin!' He laughed as he ran, panting, with the tears running down his cheeks; and in his voice I recognized the familiar love of fun and life. 'And don't forget how to laugh!'

The engine shrieked, drowning his voice. The platform, fruit stalls, advertisement boards, all slipped away; the darkness came on, the station lights twinkled, fell away, grew fainter and fainter till they they were flickering pinpoints in the distance. The stars came out. And the forest moved in around us.

We rush through the night and the wheels play a dizzy tune on the rails.

To love and be loved is the greatest happiness . . . Men and women leave the age of childhood behind, and are so busy with their buyings and sellings, their ambitions and their hopes, their loves and their hates, that they forget they once lived in a land where dreams were real. I will not forget my childhood, I shall not surrender it.

Chapter Eleven
A Far Cry from India

It was while I was living in Jersey, in the Channel Island, that I really missed India.

Jersey was a very pretty island, with wide sandy bays and rocky inlets, but it was worlds away from the land in which I had grown up. You did not see an Indian or eastern face anywhere. It was not really an English place, either, except in parts of the capital, St Helier, where some of the business houses, hotels and law firms were British-owned. The majority of the population—farmers, fishermen, councillors—spoke a French *patois* which even a Frenchman would have disowned. The island, originally French, and then for a century British, had been briefly occupied by the Germans. Now it was British again, although it had its own legislative council and made its own laws. It exported tomatoes, shrimps and Jersey cows, and imported people looking for a tax haven.

During the summer months the island was flooded with English holidaymakers. During the long, cold winter, gale-force winds swept across the Channel and the island's waterfront had a forlorn look. I knew I did not belong there and I disliked the place intensely. Within

131

days of my arrival I was longing for the languid, easy-going, mango-scented air of small-town India: the gul mohur trees in their fiery summer splendour; barefoot boys riding buffaloes and chewing on sticks of sugarcane; a hoopoe on the grass, bluejays performing aerial acrobatics; a girl's pink dupatta flying in the breeze; the scent of wet earth after the first rain; and most of all my Dehra friends.

So what on earth was I doing on an island, twelve by five miles in size, in the cold seas off Europe? Islands always sound as though they are romantic places, but take my advice, don't live on one—you'll feel deeply frustrated after a week.

I was in Jersey because my Aunt E (my mother's eldest sister) had, along with her husband and three sons, settled there a couple of years previously. So had a few other financially stable Anglo-Indian families, former residents of Poona or Bangalore; but it was not a place where young people could make a career, except perhaps in local government.

I had finished school at the end of 1950, and then for almost a year I had been loafing around in Dehra Dun, convinced that I was a writer on the strength of a couple of stories sold to *The Hindu's Sport and Pastime* (now *there* was a sports' magazine with a difference—it published my fiction!) and *The Tribune* of Ambala (Chandigarh did not exist then). My mother and stepfather finally decided to pack me off to the U.K., where, it was hoped, I would make my fortune or become Lord Mayor of London like Dick Whittington. There really wasn't much else I could have done at the time, except take a teacher's training and spend the rest of my life

teaching *As You Like It* or *Far from the Madding Crowd*
to schoolboys (in private schools) who would always have
more money than I could earn.

Anyway, my aunt had written to say that I could stay
with her in Jersey until I found my bearings, and so off I
went, in my trunk a new tweed coat and two pairs of grey
flannel trousers; also a packet of *haldi* powder, which my
aunt had particularly requested. During the voyage the
packet burst and most of my clothes were stained with
haldi.

One fine day I found myself on Ballard Pier and there
followed the long sea voyage on the P & O liner,
Strathnaver. (Built in the 1920s, it had been used as a
troopship during the War and was now a passenger liner
again.) In the early 1950s, the big passenger ships were
still the chief mode of international travel. A leisurely
cruise through the Red Sea, with a call at Aden; then
through Suez, stopping at Port Said (you had a choice
between visiting the pyramids or having a sexual
adventure in the port's back alleys); then across the
Mediterranean, with a view of Vesuvius (or was it
Stromboli?) erupting at night; a look-in at Marseilles,
where you could try out your school French and buy
naughty postcards; finally docking at Tilbury, on the
Thames estuary, just a short train ride to the heart of
London.

At Bombay, waiting for the ship's departure, I had
spent two nights in a very seedy hotel on Lamington Road,
and probably picked up the hepatitis virus there, although
I did not break out in jaundice until I was in Jersey.
Bombay never did agree with me. Now that it has been
renamed Mumbai, maybe I'll be luckier.

I liked Aden. It was unsophisticated. And although I am a lover of trees and forests, there is something about the desert (a natural desert, not a man-made one) that appeals to my solitary instincts. I am not sure that I could take up an abode permanently surrounded by sand, date-palms and camels, but it would be preferable to living in a concrete jungle—or in Jersey, for that matter!

And camels do have character.

Have I told you the story of the camel fair in Rajasthan, India's desert state? Well, there was a brisk sale in camels and the best ones fetched good prices. An elderly dealer was having some difficulty in selling a camel which, like its owner, had seen better days. It was lean, scraggy, half-blind, and moved with such a heavy roll that people were thrown off before they had gone very far.

'Who'll buy your scruffy, lame old camel?' asked a rival dealer. 'Tell me just one advantage it has over other camels.'

The elderly camel owner drew himself up with great dignity and with true Rajput pride, replied: 'There is something to be said for *character*, isn't there?'

Did I have 'character' as a boy? Probably more than I have now. I was prepared to put up with discomfort, frugal meals and even the occasional nine to five job provided I could stay up at night in order to complete my book or write a new story. Almost fifty years on, I am still leading the simple life—a good, strong bed, a desk of reasonable proportions, a coat-hanger for my one suit and a comfortable chair by the window. The rest is superstition.

*

When that ship sailed out of Aden, my ambitions were tempered by the stirrings of hepatitis within my system. That common toilet in the Lamington Road hotel, with its ever-growing uncleared mountain of human excreta, probably had something to do with it. The day after arriving at my uncle's house in Jersey, I went down with jaundice and had to spend two or three weeks in bed. It was my second attack of jaundice—I'd been hospitalized with it in Simla four years earlier—and of course I remembered that it had contributed to my father's death when he was only forty-eight. But now rest and the right diet brought about a good recovery. And as soon as I was back on my feet, I began looking for a job.

I had only three or four pounds left from my travel money, and I did not like the idea of being totally dependent on my relatives. They were a little disapproving of my writing ambitions. And sometimes they spoke disapprovingly of my mother because of her second marriage (to an 'Indian') and they were sorry for me in the way one feels sorry for an unfortunate or poor relative—simply because he or she is a relative. They were doing their duty by me, and this was noble of them; but it made me uneasy.

St Helier, the capital town and port of Jersey, was full of solicitors' offices, and I am not sure what prompted me to do the rounds of all of them, asking for a job; I think I was under the impression that solicitors were always in need of clerical assistants. But I had no luck. At seventeen, I was too young and inexperienced. One firm offered me the job of tea-boy, but as I never could brew a decent cup of tea, I felt obliged to decline the offer. Finally I ended up working for a pittance in a large grocery store,

Le Riche's, where I found myself sitting on a high stool at a high desk (like Herbert Pocket in *Great Expectations*), alongside a row of similarly positioned clerks, making up bills for despatch to the firm's regular clients.

By then it was mid-winter, and I found myself walking to work in the dark (7.30 a.m.) and walking home when it was darker still (6 p.m.)—they gave you long working hours in those days! So I did not get to see much of St Helier except at weekends.

Saturdays were half-holidays. Strolling home via a circuitous route through the old part of the town, I discovered a little cinema which ran reruns of old British comedies. And here, for a couple of bob, I made the acquaintance of performers who had come of age in the era of the music halls, and who brought to their work a broad, farcical humour that appealed to me. At school in Simla, some of them had been familiar through the pages of a favourite comic, *Film Fun*—George Formby, Sidney Howard, Max Miller ('The Cheeky Chappie', known for his double entendres), Tommy Trinder, Old Mother Riley (really a man dressed up as a woman), Laurel and Hardy and many others.

I disliked Le Riche's store. My fellow junior clerk was an egregious fellow who never stopped picking his nose. The senior clerk was interested only in the racing results from England. There were a couple of girls who drooled over the latest pop stars. I don't remember much about this period except that when King Geroge V died, we observed a minute's silence. Then back to our ledgers.

George V was a popular monarch, a quiet self-effacing man, and much respected because he had stayed in London through the Blitz when, every night for months, bombs had rained on the city. I thought he deserved more than a minute's silence. In India we observed whole holidays when almost any sort of dignitary or potentate passed away. But here it was 'The King is dead. Long live the Queen!' And then, 'Stop dreaming, Bond. Get on with those bills.'

The sea itself was always comforting and on holidays or summer evenings I would walk along the seafront, watching familiar rocks being submerged or exposed, depending on whether the tide was coming in or going out. On Sundays I would occasionally go down to the beach (St Helier's was probably the least attractive of Jersey's beaches, but it was only a short walk from my aunt's house) and sometimes I'd walk out with the tide until I came to a group of prominent rocks, and there I'd sunbathe in solitary and naked splendour. Not since the year of my father's death had I been such a loner.

I could swim a little but I was no Johnny Weissmuller, and I took care to wade back to dry land once the tide started turning. Only recently a couple had been trapped on those rocks; their bodies had been washed ashore the next day. At high tide I loved to watch the sea rushing against the sea wall, sending sprays of salt water into my face. Winter gales were frequent and I liked walking into the wind, just leaning against it. Sometimes it was strong enough to support me and I fell into its arms. It wasn't as much fun with the wind behind you, for then it propelled you along the road in a most undignified fashion, so that you looked like Charlie Chaplin in full flight.

Back in the little attic room which I had to myself, I started putting together a novel of sorts, based on the diaries I had kept during that last year in Dehra Dun. It remained a journal but I began to fill in details, trying to capture the sights, sounds and smells of that little corner of India which I had known so well. And I tried to recreate the nature and character of some of my friends—Somi, Ranbir, Kishen—and the essence of that calf-love I'd felt for Kishen's mother. I could have left it as a journal, but in that case it would not have found a publisher. In the 1950s, no publisher would have been interested in the sentimental diaries of an unknown 17-year-old. So it had to be turned into a novel. I had no title for it then, but one day it would be called *The Room on the Roof.*

Chapter Twelve

Three Jobs in Jersey

I was fortunate to discover the Jersey Library, and at this time I went through almost everything of Tagore's that had been published in those early Macmillan editions— *The Crescent Moon*, *The Gardener* and most of the plays—as well as Rumer Godden's Indian novels—*The River, Black Narcissus, Breakfast at the Nickolides*. And there was a Bengali writer, Sudhin Ghosh, who'd written a couple of enchanting memoirs of his childhood in rural Bengal—*And Gazelles Leaping* and *Cradle in the Clouds*; it's hard to find them now.

Jean Renoir's film of *The River* was released in 1952, and as I sat watching it in a St Helier cinema, waves of nostalgia flowed over me. I went to see it about five times. After three months with Le Riche's I found a job as an assistant to a travel agent, a single woman in her mid-thirties, who was opening an office in Jersey for Thomas Cook and Sons, the famous travel agency for whom she had been working in London. She was an efficient woman but jumpy, and she smoked a lot to calm her nerves. Although I abhorred the smoking habit, I was always finding myself in the company of heavy smokers—first my mother and stepfather, now Miss Manning, and in later years it was to be friends like William Matheson, Ganesh Saili and Victor Banerjee.

Miss Manning did not remove the cigarette from her lips even when she was on the phone to her London office. Her end of the conversation went something like this: 'Puff-puff—A double-room at the Seaview, did you say?—puff, suck—Separate beds or twin beds?—draw, suck, puff—Separate. They've always had separate beds, you say. Okay, puff—They're from South Africa?—puff—This hotel has a colour bar. Oh, they're white—puff—white-white or off-white?'

Colour-conscious Jersey did not encourage dark-skinned tourists from the Asian, African or American continents. I don't think Thomas Cook had any policy on this matter, but we were constantly being told by Jersey hotels that they did not take people of 'colour'. Multi-cultural Britain was still some twenty-five years away.

Miss Manning wasn't bothered by these (to her) trifles. She was having an affair with a man who sold renovated fire extinguishers. They spent the afternoons together in his rooms, a time of day when the only fires he attempted to extinguish were those raging in Miss Manning's heaving bosom. Nor could he do anything to reduce her smoking. He came to the office on one or two occasions and tried to talk me into investing twenty-five pounds in his business. I'd be part-owner of ten fire extinguishers, he told me. He was quite persuasive, but as my savings did not exceed seven pounds at the time, I could not take up his offer. He bought discarded fire extinguishers and put new life into them, he told me. They were as good as new.

So was Miss Manning, after several afternoon sessions in his rooms.

But Thomas Cook weren't happy. For several hours every day I was left in sole charge of the office, taking calls from London and booking people into the island's hotels. I couldn't help but confuse twin beds with double-beds, and was frequently putting elderly couples who hadn't slept together for years into double-beds, while forcibly separating those who couldn't have enough of each other. Miss Manning did her best to educate me in this matter of beds but I was a slow learner.

Beds could be changed around, but when I booked a group of Brazilian samba dancers into a hotel meant for 'whites only', I was fired. Later I heard that Miss Manning had been recalled to London. And her gentleman friend ran foul of the local authorities for passing off his re-charged extinguishers under his own brand name.

My next job was a more congenial one. This was in the public health department. Situated near the St Helier docks, it was a twenty-minute walk from my aunt's house—over the brow of a sometimes gale-swept hill, and down to a broad esplanade in the port area. My fellow clerks, all older than me, were a friendly, good-humoured lot, and I was to work under them as a junior clerk for more than a year.

One of them, Mr Bromley, helped me buy a new typewriter—a small Royal portable, which we saw in a department store window in town. It was priced at nineteen pounds. I had only five pounds at the time, but Mr Bromley gave me the rest and I paid it back in instalments, one pound at a time. He was a Yorkshireman who had come to work in Jersey in order to improve his health; he had a weak chest, and the cold and damp of Yorkshire did not suit him. The Channel Islands were sunnier than England. But not sunny enough for me.

I found Jersey cold in the winter. It did not snow but those gales went right through you, and my sports coat (I had no overcoat) did not really keep the cold out.

Still, there was something quite stirring, electrifying about those gales. One evening, feeling moody and dissatisfied, I deliberately went for a walk in the thick of a gale, taking the road along the seafront. The wind howled about me, almost carrying me with it along the promenade; and as it was high tide, the waves came crashing over the sea wall, stinging my face with their cold spray. It was during the walk I resolved that I was going to be a writer, come hell or high water, and that in order to do so I would have to leave Jersey and live and work in London.

This resolve was further strengthened when, a few days later, I happened to quarrel with my uncle over an entry I had made in my diary.

Keeping a diary or journal is something that I have done fitfully over the years, and sometimes it is no more than a notebook of ideas and impressions which go into the making of essays or stories. But when I am lonely or troubled it takes the form of a confessional, and this is what it was at the time. My uncle happened to come across it among my books. I don't think he was deliberately prying but he glanced through it and came across a couple of entries in which I had expressed my resentment over the very colonial attitudes that still prevailed in my uncle's family. He was a South Indian Christian, my aunt an Anglo-Indian, and yet they were champions of Empire!

This was their own business, of course, and they had a right to their views—but what I did resent was their criticism of the fact that I had young Indian friends who wrote to me quite regularly. They wanted me to forget these ties and be more British in my preferences and attitudes. Their own children had acquired English accents while I still spoke *chi-chi!*

I forget the exact words of my diary entry (I threw it away afterwards); but my uncle was offended and took me to task. I accused him of going through my personal letters and papers. Although things quietened down the next day, I had resolved to make a move.

I had saved about twelve pounds from my salary, and after giving a week's notice to the public health department, I packed my rather battered suitcase and took the cross-Channel ferry to Plymouth. A few hours later I was in London.

The cheapest place to stay was a student's hostel and I spent a few nights in the cheapest one I could find. The day after my arrival I went to the employment exchange and took the first job that was offered. I had grown quite used to changing jobs—this was my fourth or fifth in eighteen months!—and it didn't seem to matter what I did, provided it gave me enough to pay for my board and lodging and left me free to write on holidays and in the evenings.

I was alone and I was lonely but I was not afraid.

Chapter Thirteen

And Another in London

Looking back on the three years I spent in London, I realize that it must have been the most restless period of my life, judging from the number of lodging houses and residential districts I lived in—Belsize Park, Haverstock Hill, Swiss Cottage, Tooting and a couple of other places whose names I have forgotten. I don't quite know why but I was never long in any one boarding house. And unlike a Graham Greene character, I wasn't trying to escape from sinister pursuers. Unless you could call Nirdosh a sinister pursuer.

This good-hearted girl, the sister of a former schoolmate, took it into her head that I needed a sister, and fussed over me so much, and followed me about so relentlessly that I was forced to flee my Glenmore Road lodgings and move to south London (Tooting) for a month. I preferred north London because it was more cosmopolitan, with a growing population of Indian, African and continental students. I tried living in a students' hostel for a time but the food was awful and there was absolutely no privacy, so I moved back into a bedsitter and took my meals at various snack bars and small cafés. There was a nice place near Swiss Cottage where I could have a glass or two of sherry with a light supper, and after this I would walk back to my room and write a few pages of my novel.

My meals were not very substantial and I must have been suffering from some form of malnutrition because my right eye started clouding over and my sight was partially affected. I had to go into hospital for some time. The condition was diagnosed as Eale's Disease, a rare tubercular condition of the eye, and I felt quite thrilled that I could count myself among the 'greats' who had also suffered from this disease in some form or another—Keats, the Brontes, Stevenson, Katherine Mansfield, Ernest Dowson—and I thought, If only I could write like them, I'd be happy to live with a consumptive eye!

But the disease proved curable (for a time, anyway), and I went back to my job at Photax on Charlotte Street, totting up figures in heavy ledgers. Adding machines were just coming in but my employers were quite happy with their old ledgers—and so was I. I became quite good at adding pounds, shillings and pence, for hours, days, weeks, months on end. And quite contented too, provided I wasn't asked to enter the higher realms of mathematical endeavour. Maths was never my forte, although I kept reminding myself that Lewis Caroll, one of my all-time favourites, also wrote books on mathematics.

This mundane clerical job did not prevent me from pursuing the literary life, although for most of the time it was a solitary pursuit—wandering the streets of London and the East End in search of haunts associated with Dr Johnson, Dickens and his characters, W.W. Jacobs,

Jerome K. Jerome, George and Weedon Grossmith—Barrie's Kensington Gardens; Dickens' dockland; Gissing's mean streets; Fleet Street; old music halls; Soho and its Greek and Italian restaurants.

In these latter I could picture the melancholic 1890s poets, especially Ernest Dowson writing love poems to the vivacious waitress who was probably unaware of his presence. For a time I went through my Dowson period—wistful, dreamy, wallowing in a sense of loss and failure. I had even memorized some of his verses, such as these lovely lines:

> They are not long, the days of wine and roses:
> Out of a misty dream
> Our path emerges for a while, then closes
> Within a dream.

Poor Dowson, destined to die young and unfulfilled. A minor poet, dismissed as inconsequential by the critics, and yet with us still, a singer of sad but exquisite songs.

*

Although for my first six months in London I did live in a garret and an unhealthy one at that, I did not really see myself in the role of the starving poet. The first thing I did was to look for a job, and I took the first that was offered—the office job at Photax, a small firm selling photographic components and accessories. A little way down the road was the Scala Theatre, and as soon as I had saved enough for a theatre ticket (theatre-going wasn't expensive in those days), I went to see the annual

146

Christmas production of *Peter Pan*, which I'd read as a play when I was going through the works of Barrie in my school library. This production had Margaret Lockwood as Peter. She had been Britain's most popular film star in the forties and she was still pretty and vivacious. I think Captain Hook was played by Donald Wolfit, better known for his portrayal of Svengali.

My colleagues in Photax, though not in the least literary, were a friendly lot. There was my fellow clerk, Ken, who shared his marmite sandwiches with me. There was Maisie of the auburn hair, who was constantly being rung up by her boyfriends. And there was Clarence, who was slightly effeminate and known to frequent the gay bars in Soho. (Except that the term 'gay' hadn't been invented yet.) And there was our head clerk, Mr Smedly, who'd been in the Navy during the War, and was a musical-theatre buff. We would often discuss the latest musicals—*Guys and Dolls, South Pacific, Paint Your Wagon, Pal Joey*—big musicals which used to run for months, even years.

The window opposite my desk looked out on a huge cinema hoarding, and it was always an event when a new poster went up on it. Weeks before the film was released, there was a poster of Judy Garland in her comeback film, *A Star is Born*, and I can still remember the publicity headline: 'Judy, the world is waiting for your sunshine!' And, of course, there was Marilyn Monroe in *Niagara*, with Marilyn looking much bigger than the waterfall, and that fine actor, Joseph Cotten, nowhere in sight.

My heart, though, was not in the Photax office. I had no ambitions to become head clerk or even to learn the intricacies of the business. It was a nine-to-five job, giving me just enough money to live on (six pounds a week, in fact), while I scribbled away of an evening, working on my second (or was it third?) draft of my novel. The title was the only thing about it that did not change. It was *The Room on the Roof* from the beginning.

How I worked at that book! I was always being asked to put things in or take things out. At first the publishers suggested that it needed 'filling out'. When I filled it out, I was told that it was now a little too descriptive and would I prune it a bit? And what started out as a journal and then became a first-person narrative finally ended up in the third person. But editors only made suggestions; they did not tamper with your language or style. And the 'feel' of the story—my love for India and my friends in particular—was ever present, running through it like a vein of gold.

Much of the publishers' uncertain and contradictory suggestions stemmed from the fact they relied heavily on their readers' recommendations. A 'reader' was a well-known writer or critic who was asked (and paid) to give his opinion on a book. *The Room on the Roof* was sent to the celebrated literary critic, Walter Allen, who said I was a 'born writer' and likened me to Sterne, but also said I should wait a little longer before attempting a novel. Another reader, Laurie Lee (the author of *Cider with Rosie*), said he had enjoyed the story but that it would be a gamble to publish it.[*]

Fortunately, Andre Deutsch was the sort of publisher

---

[*] Some of the correspondence (or that which has survived) in connection with this first novel is given in *Notes and Letters*. It might be of interest to other budding authors.

who was ready to take a risk with a new, young author; so instead of rejecting the book, he bought an option on it, which meant that he could sit on it for a couple of years until he had made up his mind!

My mentor at this time was Diana Athill, Deutsch's editor and junior partner. She was at least ten years older than me but we became good friends. She invited me to her flat for meals and sometimes accompanied me to the pictures or the theatre. She was tall, auburn-haired and attractive in a sort of angular English way, but our relationship was purely platonic. It hadn't occurred to me to try and make love to an older woman. I saw her as a literary person (which she undoubtedly was) and not as a sex object. She was fond of me. She could see I was suffering from malnutrition and as she was a good cook (in addition to being a good editor), she shared her very pleasant and wholesome meals with me. There is nothing better than good English food, no matter what the French or Italians or Chinese may say. A lamb chop, a fish nicely fried, cold meat with salad, or shepherd's pie, or even an Irish stew, are infinitely more satisfying than most of the stuff served in continental or Far Eastern restaurants. I suppose it's really a matter of childhood preferences. I still fancy a kofta curry because koftas were what I enjoyed most in Granny's house. And oh, for one of Miss Kellner's meringues—but no one seems to make them any more.

I really neglected myself during those three years I spent in London. Never much of a cook, I was hard put to fry myself an egg every morning before rushing off to catch the tube for Tottenham Court Road, a journey of about twenty-five minutes. In the lunch break I would stroll across to a snack bar and have the inevitable baked beans-on-toast. There wasn't time for a more substantial meal, even if I could afford it. In the evenings I could indulge myself a little, with a decent meal in a quiet café; but most of the time I existed on snacks. No wonder I ended up with a debilitating disease!

Perhaps the most relaxing period of my London life was the month I spent in the Hampstead General Hospital, which turned out to be a friendly sort of place.

I was sent there for my Eale's disease, and the treatment consisted of occasional cortisone injections to my right eye. But I was allowed—even recommended—a full diet, supplemented by a bottle of Guinness with my lunch. They felt that I needed a little extra nourishment—wise doctors, those!

The bottle of Guinness made me the envy of the ward, but I made myself popular by sharing the drink with neighbouring patients when the nurses weren't looking. One nurse was a ravishing South American beauty, and half the ward fell in love with her.

It was a general ward and one ailing patient—a West Indian from Trinidad—felt that he was being singled out for experimentation by the doctors. He set up a commotion whenever he had to be given a rather painful lumbar puncture. I would sit on his bed and try to calm him down, and he became rather dependent on my moral support, insisting on my presence whenever he was being examined or treated.

While I was in hospital, I got in a lot of reading (with one eye), wrote a short story, and received visitors in style. They ranged from my colleagues at Photax, to Diana Athill, my would-be publisher, to some of my Indian friends in Hampstead, to my latest landlady, a motherly sort who'd lost some of her children in Hitler's persecution of the Jews.

When I left the hospital I was richer by a few pounds, having saved my salary and been treated free on account of the National Health Scheme. The spots had cleared from my eyes and I'd put on some weight, thanks to the lamb chops and Guinness that had constituted my lunch.

I gave George, the West Indian, my home address, although I did not expect to see him again. A few months later I found him on my doorstep, fully recovered. We repaired to a nearby pub and drank rum. He invited me to a calypso party in Camden Town, and when I arrived I found I was the only 'white' in a gathering of some forty handsome black men and women, all determined to eat, drink and be merry into the early hours of the morning. I fell asleep on a settee halfway through the party. Someone fell asleep on top of me.

I met George occasionally (he worked for British Rail), and there were one or two more wild parties; but before I could become a part of the calypso scene I met Vu-Phuong, and once again my life took on a different direction.

Thanh, a Vietnamese part-time student, befriended me because he thought I could improve his English. Later, when he discovered that I spoke more like an Indian than an Englishman, he decided to drop me; but for a couple of months I received the benefits of his cooking, Vietnamese dishes coming to him quite naturally as his uncle owned a restaurant in Paris. I never could learn to use chopsticks, and to his disgust consumed my rice and noodles with spoon, fork or fingers.

It was Thanh who introduced me to a Vietnamese girl call Vu-Phuong, and I promptly fell in love with her.

At that age it did not take long for me to fall in love with anyone, and Vu was the sort of girl—pretty, soft-spoken, demure—who could enslave me without any apparent effort.

She was happy to accompany me on walks across Hampstead Heath and over Primrose Hill. It was summer time and the grass smelt sweet and was good to lie upon. We lay close to each other and watched boys flying kites. No one bothered us. She put her hand in mine. I walked her home and she made tea for me, and she told me my fortune with playing cards. I can't remember what the cards foretold; I wasn't paying much attention to them.

We went about together. She said she looked upon me as a friend, a brother (fatal word!), and would depend upon me for many things. When she went away for a fortnight, I was desolate. It was only as far as a farm in Berkshire where she had joined some other girl students picking strawberries. On a Sunday I took a train to Newbury and then a small branch line to the village of Kintbury—a pretty little place with an old inn, a couple of small shops and plenty of farmland. I had Vu's address, and after lunching at the inn, I set off for the farm where Vu and her friends were working. It was a lovely summer's day, and my first walk in the English countryside.

It took me back to a favourite story, H.E. Bates' *Alexander*, and some of his Uncle Silas tales. Although I had walked all over London, this was different, and I wish now that I had spent more time in the country and less in the city.

Vu seemed happy to see me but she was equally happy among her friends—those fresh-faced, healthy-looking English schoolgirls—and obviously enjoyed living on the farm and picking strawberries. I don't suppose there could have been a better way of earning enough money for college and hostel fees. I walked back to Kintbury alone and reached Charing Cross station late at night. I spent an hour in one of those little news theatres which interspersed newsreels with cartoon shows; supped off station coffee and sandwiches; and then took the last train to Swiss Cottage.

Two or three weeks later I asked Vu if she'd marry me. She didn't say yes and she didn't say no. Nor did she ask me if I had any prospects, because it was obvious I had none. But she did say she would have to talk to her parents about it and they were in Haiphong, in North Vietnam, and she hadn't heard from them for several months. The war in Vietnam had just started and it was to last a long time.

I had to be patient, it seemed, very patient.

Because the next I heard from Vu was through a postcard from Paris saying she was staying with her sister for a time and they would be returning to Vietnam together to see their parents.

I kept that postcard for a long time. The stamp bore a picture of Joan of Arc looking like Michele Morgan in one of her early films.

The day I received it I took a day off from the office and went to a pub and drank several large brandies. They didn't do me any good, so I switched to Jamaica rum and all that it did was make me think of Vu and, of course, I never saw her again.

153

Chapter Fourteen

Return to Dehra

After the insularity of Jersey, London was liberating. Theatres, cinemas, bookshops, museums, libraries helped further my self-education. Not once did I give serious thought to joining a college and picking up a degree. In any case, I did not have the funds, and there was no one to sponsor me. Instead, I had to join the vast legion of the world's workers. But Kensington Gardens, Regent's Park, Hampstead Heath and Primrose Hill gave me the green and open spaces that I needed in order to survive. In many respects London was a green city. My forays into the East End were really in search of literary landmarks.

And yet something was missing from my life. Vu-Phuong had come and gone like the breath of wind after which she had been named. And there was no one to take her place.

The affection, the camaraderie, the easy-going pleasures of my Dehra friendships; the colour and atmosphere of India; the feeling of *belonging*—these things I missed . . .

Even though I had grown up with a love for the English language and its literature, even though my forefathers

were British, Britain was not really my place. I did not
belong to the bright lights of Piccadilly and Leicester
Square; or, for that matter, to the apple orchards of Kent
or the strawberry fields of Berkshire. I belonged, very
firmly, to peepal trees and mango groves; to sleepy little
towns all over India; to hot sunshine, muddy canals, the
pungent scent of marigolds; the hills of home; spicy
odours, wet earth after summer rain, neem pods bursting;
laughing brown faces; and the intimacy of human contact.

Human contact! That was what I missed most. It was
not to be found in the office where I worked, or in my
landlady's house, or in any of the learned societies which
I had joined, or even in the pubs into which I sometimes
wandered . . . The freedom to touch someone without being
misunderstood. To take someone by the hand as a mark
of affection rather than desire. Or even to know desire.
And fulfilment. To be among strangers without feeling
like an outsider. For, in India there are no strangers . . .

I had been away for over three years but the bonds were
as strong as ever, the longing to return had never left me.

How I expected to make a living in India when I
returned is still something of a mystery to me. You did not
just walk into the nearest employment exchange to find a
job waiting for you. I had no qualifications. All I could do
was write and I was still a novice at that. If I set myself
up as a freelance writer and bombarded every magazine
in the country, I could probably eke out a livelihood. At
that time there were only some half a dozen English
language magazines in India and almost no book
publishers (except for a handful of educational presses left
over from British days). The possibilities were definitely
limited; but this did not deter me. I had confidence in

myself (too much, perhaps), plenty of guts (my motto being, 'Never despair. But if you do, work on in despair.'). And, of course, all the optimism of youth.

As Diana Athill and Andre Deutsch kept telling me they would publish *The Room* one day (I had finally put my foot, or rather, my pen, down and refused to do any more work on it), I wheedled a fifty-pound advance out of them, this being the standard advance against royalties in 1953. Out of this princely sum I bought a ticket for Bombay on the *S.S. Batory*, a Polish passenger liner which had seen better days. There was a fee for a story I'd sold to the BBC and some money saved from my Photax salary; and with these amounts I bought a decent-looking suitcase and a few presents to take home.

I did not say goodbye to many people—just my office colleagues who confessed that they would miss my imitations of Sir Harry Lauder; and my landlady, to whom I gave my Eartha Kitt records—and walked up the gangway of the *Batory* on a chilly day early in March.

Soon we were in the warmer waters of the Mediterranean and a few days later in the even warmer Red Sea. It grew gloriously hot. But the *Batory* was a strange ship, said to be jinxed. A few months earlier, most of its Polish crew had sought political asylum in Britain. And now, as we passed through the Suez Canal, a crew member jumped overboard and was never seen again. Hopefully he'd swum ashore.

Then, when we were in the Arabian Sea, we had to get out of our bunks in the middle of the night for the ship's alarm bells were ringing and we thought the *Batory* was sinking. As there had been no lifeboat drill and no one had any idea of how a lifebelt should be worn, there was a certain amount of panic. Cries of 'Abandon ship!' mingled with shouts of 'Man overboard!' and 'Women and children first!'—although there were no signs of women and children being given that privilege. Finally it transpired that a passenger, tipsy on too much Polish vodka, had indeed fallen overboard. A lifeboat was lowered and the ship drifted around for some time; but whether or not the passenger was rescued, we were not told. Nor did I discover his (or her) identity. Whatever tragedy had occurred had been swallowed up in the immensity of the darkness and the sea.

The saga of the *Batory* was far from over.

No sooner had the ship docked at Bombay's Ballard Pier than a fire broke out in the hold. Most of the passengers lost their heavy luggage. Fortunately, my suitcase and typewriter were both with me and these I clung to all the way to the Victoria Terminus and all the way to Dehra Dun. I knew it would be some time before I could afford more clothes or another typewriter.

When the train drew into Delhi I found that my stepfather had come to meet me. This was decent of him and it was the beginning of a more understanding relationship. He told me that he and my mother were planning to move to Delhi.

He travelled with me to Dehra Dun, and on Dehra's small platform I found Dipi waiting to greet me. (Somi and Haripal were now in Calcutta.)

Dipi had come on his cycle.

I told my stepfather I'd join him at home and put my suitcase and typewriter into his latest second-hand car. Then I got up on the crossbar of Dipi's bike and he took me home in style, through the familiar streets of the town that had so shaped my life.

The Odeon was showing an old Bogart film; the small roadside cafés were open; the bougainvillaea were a mass of colour; the mango blossoms smelt sweet; Dipi chattered away; and the girls looked prettier than ever.

And I was twenty-one that year.

Envoi

Letter to My Father

My dear Dad,

Last week I decided to walk from the Dilaram Bazaar to Rajpur, a walk I hadn't undertaken for many years. It's only about five miles, a long, straight, tree-lined road, houses most of the way, but here and there open spaces where there are fields and patches of Sal forest. The road hasn't changed much, but there is far more traffic than there used to be, which makes it noisy and dusty, detracting from the prettiness of the surrounding countryside. Recently, when a schoolboy asked me to describe the Doon Valley in one sentence, I could only say: 'A paradise that *might* have been . . .'

All the same I enjoyed the walk—enjoyed the cool breeze that came down from the hills—the rich variety of trees. The splashes of colour where bougainvillaea trailed over porches and verandahs—enjoyed the passing cyclists and bullock carts, for they were reminders of the days when cars, trucks and buses were the exception rather than the rule.

159

A little way above the Dilaram Bazaar, just where the canal goes under the road, stands the old house we used to know as Melville Hall, where three generations of Melvilles had lived. It is now a government office and looks dirty and neglected. Beside it still stands the little cottage or guest house where you stayed for a few weeks while the separation from my mother was being finalized. Then I went to live with you in Delhi.

At that time you were a guest of the Melvilles and I was at the convent in Mussoorie, so I did not share the cottage with you, although I was to share a number of rooms, tents and RAF hutments with you during the next two or three years. But of course I knew the Melvilles—I would visit them during school holidays in the years after you had gone. One of them was particularly kind to me. This was Mrs Chill—she'd lost her husband in an accident just after their marriage, and had never married again. But I always found her cheerful and good-natured, sending me presents on my birthday and at Christmas. The kindest people are often those who have come through testing personal tragedies.

A young man on a bicycle stops beside me and asks if I remember him.

'Not with that bushy moustache,' I confess.

'Sanjay, from Sisters Bazaar.'

'Yes, of course.' And I do remember him, although it must be about ten years since we last met. He was just a schoolboy then. Now, he tells me, he's a teacher. Not very well paid, as he works for a small private school owned by a property dealer. But better than being unemployed, he says. I have to agree.

'You're a good teacher, I'm sure, Sanjay. And, perhaps,

one day it will be a noble profession again.'

He looks pleased as he cycles away.

When I see boys on bicycles, I am always taken back to my boyhood days in Dehra. The roads were then ideal for cyclists. Somi on his bicycle, riding down this very road in the light spring rain, gave me the opening scene for *The Room on the Roof,* written a couple of years after I'd said goodbye to Somi and Dehra and even, for a time, India.

That's how I remember him best, on his bicycle, wearing shorts, turban slightly askew, almost always a song on his lips. Tapas Guha captures the mood in his lyrical cover illustration for the Penguin India edition of *The Room* and *Vagrants in the Valley.*

Somi was just twelve or thirteen; I was two or three years older, but I wasn't much of a bicycle rider, although I'd love to have written a book like Saroyan's autobiographical *Bicycle Rider in Beverly Hills.* I was always falling off the cycle when I was supposed to dismount gracefully. One day I went sailing into a buffalo cart and fractured my forearm. Some forty years later, when Dr Murti, now a senior citizen, met me at a local function, he recalled how he had set my arm after the accident. It was so pleasant meeting him again that I forbore from telling him that the arm was still crooked!

Strictly an earth man, I have never really felt at ease with my feet off the ground. That's why I've been a walking person for most of my life. In planes, on ships, even in lifts, panic sets in.

As it did on that occasion when I was four or five, and you decided to give me a treat by taking me in a dhow across the Gulf of Kutch. Five minutes on that swinging, swaying, sailing ship was enough for me; I became so hysterical that I had to be taken off and rowed back to port. Not that the rowing boat was much better.

And, then, my mother thought I should go up in one of those four-winged aeroplanes, a Tiger Moth it was called—there's a photograph of it somewhere among my mementos—one of those contraptions that fell out of the sky at the least provocation. I think you could assemble them at home! Anyway, in this too I kicked and screamed with such abandon that the poor pilot (a relative of the ruling Jamnagar family) had to be content with taxiing around the airfield and dropping me off at the first opportunity. That same plane with the same pilot crashed a couple of months later, only reinforcing my fears about machines that would not stay firmly on the ground.

In time I grew out of most of my phobias, but I still take the stairs in preference to the lift.

*

To return to Somi, he was one of those friends I never saw again as an adult, so he remains transfixed in my memory as eternal youth, dream-bright, unchanging . . . Meeting boyhood friends after long intervals can often be disappointing, even disconcerting. Mere survival leaves its mark. Success is even more disfiguring. Those who get to the top of a profession, or reach the pinnacles of power, usually have to pay a heavy price for it.

I have often dreamt of Somi, and it is always the same dream . . . We meet in a fairground, set up on the old parade ground. In the dream I am a man but he is still a boy. We wander through the fairground, enjoying all that it has to offer, in much the same way that we have enjoyed all that life had to offer.

Is that heaven—the perfect place with the perfect companion? And if you and I meet again, Dad, will you look the same, and will I be a small boy or an old man? And what happened to all those missing years?

Love is undying; of that I feel certain. I mean deep, abiding, cherishing love. The love that gives protection even as you, my guardian angel, gave me protection long after you had gone—and continue to give this very day . . .

A love beyond Death—a love that makes Life alive!

Notes and Letters

A Young Writer and His First Publisher[*]

January 16th, 1953

Dear Mr Bond,

Thank you for your letter. I am glad that our rejection of *The Room on the Roof* discouraged you so little.

Yes, send it again, or bring it, when you have finished working on it. The only sense in which I am now 'regretting my interest' is that I cannot help feeling '*Supposing* we still turn it down, for one reason or another, when he has put so much more work in on it, how much worse that will be for all concerned'. That naturally makes me feel a little apprehensive. But you realize, no doubt, that it might happen? And as we do really feel that a reconsideration would be worthwhile it would be a pity not to disregard the risk of disappointment.

---

[*] The correspondence with Diana Athill is courtesy Boston University's Special Collections Library. Reproduced here are some of the letters exchanged between the author and Diana Athill.

May I say that I admire your determination to re-shape this book? It will be a difficult thing to do, and I imagine that it must be rather painful to undertake such a major operation on one's first-born.

Yours sincerely,
Diana Athill

Ruskin Bond, Esq.,
Southdene
Regent Road, St Helier,
Jersey, C.I.

*

March 6th 1954

Ruskin Bond, Esq.,
124 Haverstock Hill,
London N.W.I.

My dear Ruskin,

I have read *The Room* (and it *must* be *The Room*—it is the inevitable title for it), and I like it. I gave it to someone else to read yesterday, and they brought it back to me saying 'I think it's a lovely story'. Andre hasn't read it yet, however, so you will just have to make do with this much at present.

I am *not* without criticism, however, and two I can give you straight away. 1. The end is a bit too fairy-tale. The coincidence of your meeting with Kamini by the river strains the credulity at a point when it is absolutely vital that it should not be strained. I thought that this could be avoided fairly easily by making something like this happen: Perhaps a neighbour to the house where she had been with her mother in Hardwar could chip in and say that *she* had an idea where the girl might be found—she had felt sorry for her, and had tried to help her, but Kamini had not accepted it (excepting, perhaps, for once or twice taking food from her) and had slipped off into the town: but she had seen her about occasionally, and thought that she often hung about the steps to the river . . . You could still be pretty hopeless about finding her, and so have the hopeless feeling of page 121, but when you *did* find her it would not make the reader feel 'how very convenient!' in that disturbing way. *

The other thing is that you have been too ruthless in your pruning away of inessentials. What you have done, in fact, is write as though your medium was the short story, not the novel. You don't give time enough time to pass in! (I'm not sure that that isn't rather a meaningless remark!) What I mean is, that some incidents and people could be, perhaps, a little enlarged, so that the reader had time to settle down in them. Particularly, this applies where you first go to live with Somi. This is a crux point, new life, and you dismiss that week in a page or two. I think you could enlarge here quite a lot, with benefit. Somehow the feeling of strangeness and excitement at the small things being different, the eating and the sleeping and the washing . . . You are taking your reader from one world (superficially speaking) into another, as well as yourself, and you must allow them more time to get the feel of it.

---

* In this draft, Kishen had become Kamini (purely a literary sex-change), but reverted to Kishen in the final draft.

I wonder what you will feel about that. Does it make sense to you?

I shall try very hard to get you the final decision as soon as possible, and no doubt we'll be talking more about the book soon. Meanwhile, I do think you have done wonders.

Yours
Diana

P.S. I'll tell you one thing that I missed—the original Kapoor family. You'll begin to wonder why I don't sit down and write the book myself, soon; but couldn't Somi's family have such neighbours, who could come into that chapter. Kishen could still be their spoilt son. Your pupils rather materialise out of thin air, as it stands, and they would be more explained if you had two families backing you as a teacher, and telling people about you. And that old drunk father was a good solid character—an excellent filler in of atmosphere and background.

*

Wednesday

My dear Ruskin,

I have just had posted off the *Room*, to Laurie Lee the poet, who has agreed to read certain books for us. It is best, I feel, to get a brand new opinion on the new version, given without any bias one way or another—and Laurie is a nice perceptive man.

I've been through it myself and am charmed by the new

bits. They are a huge improvement in my view—and so smoothly done that they don't stick out in the least as additions.

Yours,
Diana

*

My dear R.

L.L.'s verdict was 'it would be a gamble to publish this but I wouldn't blame you if you took it'. His criticisms were that you lacked dramatic sense and that there was something scrappy and incomplete about the book. But he was much impressed by its poetic qualities, the sensitiveness of your writing, the sanity of your outlook. This has put Andre into a state of great split-mindedness. I don't mind telling you that I am going to fight tooth and nail for it, and after Whitsun I will back A. against a wall and *force* a decision out of him before the week is up. This I promise, and may I drop dead if I fail. I'm terribly glad to hear that someone else has got onto you—most gratifying. The talk was excellent.*

I'm in a flat spin. Leave for my holiday on the eighteenth—am away this weekend and next. Suggest next Wednesday the 9th for the Japanese film, which I would like to see. I honestly believe it's the only evening I can make, which sounds awful, but there you are.

Yours
D.

* A talk I did for the BBC.

14-Glenmore Road,
Belsize Park,
London N.W.3.

August 5th, 1953

Andre Deutsch Ltd.,
12 Thayer Street,
Manchester Square, W.I.

Dear Miss Athill and Mr Deutsch,

On Saturday the 30th of May you were kind enough to offer to buy an option on my next book, and I was told I would receive the contract within a week. In your letter of the 17th June you regretted that the contract had not been despatched earlier because of business pressure, and mentioned that it would soon be on its way. As you had sent the MS of *The Room on the Roof* to New York, because of a London representative's enthusiasm, I fully appreciated the delay; and was not over-anxious when June turned to July, and July to August, and still no contract and still no news.

However, August 1953, is a long way off from December 1952, when I first came to you, and though I am aware and appreciative of the many ways in which I have benefited from my perseverance with your firm, I now feel that I have been 'on the rack' long enough and that I deserve a final decision.

I would like to stress my appreciation of the fact that you are busy people, and that whilst I have only one book to worry about, you have scores; and I also appreciate the fact that I am very young and can therefore be made to wait. Indeed, I am only too glad to wait, provided I know there is something to wait for.

I want to know where I stand, that is all. After I have worked and waited for almost a year, I want to know what is really happening—*if* anything is happening—and why it is happening, and why there is no contract and no news of an MS which might well be employed better elsewhere. Everything is too vague and indefinite, and this continual uncertainty does not encourage further constructive work.

I have not wanted to write this letter, because I have not wanted to hurry you, because to hurry you might have been to spoil my chances. But I must risk offending you, by asking that you please give me your final decision by the end of the month.

If this letter has already convinced you of my utter unsuitability for the role of one of your authors, I would appreciate the return of my MS of *The Room on the Roof*. I do not ask any favours. I want no friendship. I only want business.

If you have incurred any expenses on my behalf, such as the payment of fees to readers, please send me a bill for the same.

Yours sincerely,
Ruskin Bond

*

11th August, 1953

Dear Ruskin,

How perfectly awful this is! I should have written to you weeks and weeks before explaining the delay and I feel that our pressure of business has not really been a good enough excuse. We have been very hectic though, bringing out *Witness* and Adlai Stevenson's *Speeches*.

We had to hold the contract up until we had heard from Viking Press in case their news made any modification necessary. They have now let us know that they like your book very much, but they are certainly not going to offer to publish it. Whether or not we can get a contract for an option out of them I am still not yet sure, meanwhile here is our contract with the most sincere apologies.

I wish you had not written such a very nice letter about it because it makes me feel worse. I want to know how the new novel is going and I would appreciate it if you would come round to supper next Saturday, the 5th, and tell me about it.

Yours sincerely,
Diana

* Will tell you more about this, which is not as unpromising as it sounds, when I see you.

Ruskin Bond, Esq.,
14 Glenmore Road,
Belsize Park,
London, N.W.3.

June 17th, 1954

Ruskin Bond, Esq.,
124 Haverstock Hill,
London, N.W.3.

My dear Ruskin,

I have much pleasure in enclosing a) a postal order for 2/6 which you sent us today (which, if I may say so, was silly), and b) a cheque for £50 which is the sum agreed between us in our contract of August 11th, 1953, to be paid by us on the acceptance of your manuscript.

As you can imagine, I am delighted to be able to do this before I leave for my holiday. Andre has asked me to tell you that he has certain suggestions to make about the book—his enthusiasm is not entirely unqualified—but he feels that as you and I have been the only ones involved in discussion of it so far, it would be a good idea to wait until I get back in three weeks time before going into the matter. As soon as I am home again I will get in touch with you and then you can come round and we can talk to him about it. This doesn't mean that our acceptance is conditional or anything; it is simply that he believes that there are certain points at which you might improve it and that it would be in your interest as well as in ours if you were to agree to consider this.

Yours,
Diana

P.S. HURRAH! HURRAH!! HURRAH!!! (is that how one spells it? it looks funny)

You'd better write to Andre acknowledging this (and apologising for the 2/6—
it made us rather cross!) Until July the somethingth!

*

May 26th, 1956

My dear Ruskin,

I think you'll agree that the enclosed adds up to a very gratifying 22nd birthday present, even though rather belated! One result of it is that we will never be spoken to by Wolf Mankowitz* again! I've written to Miss Scrutton,** whom I don't know, telling her how happy she has made us all by her warm and sympathetic attitude—and I wish you were here so that we could celebrate your first really smashing review (and one, let me point out, such as many novelists live all their lives without getting!). It remains to be seen what effect it has on sales—but even if it makes no material difference, what a feather in your cap!

I'm longing to see the *Leopard in the Lounge.*+ Be resolute and finish it soon.

The village holiday sounded lovely and enviable. I think I shall go back to Jugoslavia again this summer, if I can afford it, because it is far too interesting a country to be dealt with in the one short holiday I had there last year. I've got friends there now, in Belgrade (which they

---

* Wolf Mankowitz, one of Deutsch's most successful authors in the 1950s. The same reviewer was rather dismissive of his work.
** Mary Scrutton, book reviewer for *The New Statesman,* London.
\+ This novella eventually became *Time Stops at Shamli.*

173

say is one of the ugliest, dirtiest, noisiest cities in Europe), which will make it even more fun.

Barbara is off to Majorca today for a long weekend, believe it or not—wild girl. I don't know what she plans to do for her proper holiday.

Good that you liked the jacket. I'll tell Leonard.[*] And *good* about Newby[**] doing a story of yours. Thank you for saying you'll let us have the details.

Haven't seen the *I'll. Weekly*[+] yet, but am looking forward to it.

I'm in a hurry as usual. I must obviously give up any claim to be a letter writer that I ever had.

Minor reviews I'll wait to send you until we can make a more or less complete collection.

Love from
Diana

How long will it take you to live down 'Dew-drenched celandine' among your tougher friends?

*

---

[*] Leonard Rosoman. Artist and illustrator.
[**] P.H. Newby, author. Commissioned me to write stories for the BBC, when he was a producer in Talks Division.
[+] *The Illustrated Weekly of India*, then edited by C.R. Mandy, serialized *The Room on the Roof* and its sequel, *Vagrants in the Valley*.

9th April, 1957

Dear Mr Bond,

You will know , I expect, that your publisher submitted your book, *The Room on the Roof,* for the John Llewellyn Rhys Memorial Prize. Now, I don't quite know what to do with your invitation, since I hear from your publisher that you are in India, and therefore cannot possibly accept it! But I think I shall send it just the same, as it is proof that you have been chosen as one of the four finalists who are asked to the party at which the prize itself is awarded.[*]

I should like to say how interested the Selection Committee is in your work, and to add that it is not impossible that you will be hearing from us again before long.

With all best wishes for your future success,

Your sincerely,
Helen Rhys

Ruskin Bond, Esq.,
c/o Messrs. Andre Deutsch & Co.
12, 14 Carlisle St.
Soho Square,
London. W.I.

*

---

[*] I missed the party but won the prize.

175

A Note on Granny's House

This was the nearest thing to a 'family home', since no one else in the family ever owned any property.

The house on Old Survey Road was left to Granny's eldest daughter, my Aunt Emily, who promptly sold it, leaving India for good in 1948.

Over the years, I was often drawn towards the old bungalow, as it had represented a sort of port in the storm of my childhood days.

The house is still there, although now cut in half and with different owners.

Last winter, when I was in Dehra, I happened to be looking over the wall when I was recognized by the owner, Mrs Kakkar, who beckoned me in and very kindly offered me tea and biscuits. It was her father who had bought the house from my aunt.

I asked her why she had kept the shadier, darker side of the house, selling the brighter half. She said she had always been told that one of my aunts or great-aunts had hanged herself in that part of the house.

Not true, I said, no aunt of mine had ever hanged herself, although a few men may have hanged themselves on their account. I did not point out that Miss Kellner had died in the bedroom that was now Mrs Kakkar's. But Miss Kellner was too crippled to have hanged herself, unless someone did it for her.

When I left, Mrs Kakkar gave me a pomalo from one of the pomalo trees which, she said, my grandfather had planted. This was a nice gesture on her part.

I brought the pomalo home and shared it with the children in our rented cottage.

A Note on Uncle Bertie

Herbert (Bertie) Bond was my father's elder brother. For most of his adult life he worked as a foreman in the Ishapur Rifle factory. He did not marry, but in his middle years took on the responsibility of looking after a widow with seven or eight children.

[In this respect I resemble him slightly, having, in my middle years, adopted a large and ever growing family in the hills!]

I did not meet Uncle Bertie until he was in his sixties. In 1954 I tracked him down to his small bed-sitting room in Islington, and we spent a pleasant couple of hours together. The eldest of his adopted sons lived in a room above him, and very kindly brought me tea and sandwiches.

As I did not want to intrude on my uncle's personal life, I did not go out of my way to see him again, although we wrote to each other occasionally over the next few years. He loved to reminisce about his schooldays at Sanawar and told me a ghost story about Tolly's Nullah in Calcutta.

He was a short, plump man. He did not resemble my father very much. My father and his younger brother, Arthur, bore a close resemblance. Arthur died young. Their sister, Alma, was killed in an air raid over Manchester during the War.

The facsimile of my grandfather's Army service record was sent to me by my Uncle Bertie, whom I met just once. Although he was the eldest son, he survived his sister and two brothers.

The record shows that my father was born in Shahjehanpur, a small cantonment town which, coincidentally, became the setting for my novella, *A Flight of Pigeons*.

Uncle Bertie told me that his mother (my 'Calcutta Granny') was an orphan who had grown up on an indigo estate in Motihari, Bihar.

The children were all born in different places. Those were the days of Kipling's 'route marchin' soldiers—and they were certainly kept on the move!

Uncle Bertie told me that grandfather was a quiet, reclusive sort of person who never lost his temper with anyone. His favourite pastime was watching jugglers and street acrobats! I wish I had known him.

READ MORE IN PENGUIN

In every corner of the world, on every subject under the sun, Penguin represents quality and variety—the very best in publishing today.

For complete information about books available from Penguin—including Puffins, Penguin Classics and Arkana—and how to order them, write to us at the appropriate address below. Please note that for copyright reasons the selection of books varies from country to country.

In India: Please write to *Penguin Books India Pvt. Ltd. 11 Community Centre, Panchsheel Park, New Delhi 110017*

In the United Kingdom: Please write to *Dept JC, Penguin Books Ltd. Bath Road, Harmondsworth, West Drayton, Middlesex, UB7 ODA. UK*

In the United States: Please write to *Penguin USA Inc., 375 Hudson Street, New York, NY 10014*

In Canada: Please write to *Penguin Books Canada Ltd. 10 Alcorn Avenue, Suite 300, Toronto, Ontario M4V 3B2*

In Australia: Please write to *Penguin Books Australia Ltd. 487, Maroondah Highway, Ring Wood, Victoria 3134*

In New Zealand: Please write to *Penguin Books (NZ) Ltd. Private Bag, Takapuna, Auckland 9*

In the Netherlands: Please write to *Penguin Books Netherlands B.V., Keizersgracht 231 NL-1016 DV Amsterdom*

In Germany : Please write to *Penguin Books Deutschland GmbH, Metzlerstrasse 26, 60595 Frankfurt am Main, Germany*

In Spain: Please write to *Penguin Books S.A., Bravo Murillo, 19-1'B, E-28015 Madrid, Spain*

In Italy: Please write to *Penguin Italia s.r.l., Via Felice Casati 20, I-20104 Milano*

In France: Please write to *Penguin France S.A., 17 rue Lejeune, F-31000 Toulouse*

In Japan: Please write to *Penguin Books Japan. Ishikiribashi Building, 2-5-4, Suido, Tokyo 112*

In Greece: Please write to *Penguin Hellas Ltd, dimocritou 3, GR-106 71 Athens*

In South Africa: Please write to *Longman Penguin Books Southern Africa (Pty) Ltd, Private Bag X08, Bertsham 2013*